ESSENTIAL
FACTS FOR
MANAGERS

ESSENTIAL FACTS FOR MANAGERS

Published in association with British Institute of Management

BRITISH INSTITUTE OF MANAGEMENT

© 1987 Professional Publishing Ltd

First published in 1987 by Professional Publishing Ltd,
7 Swallow Place, London W1R 8AB

First published in 1988 by Kogan Page Ltd,
120 Pentonville Road, London N1 9JN
in association with British Institute of Management,
Management House, Cottingham Road, Corby, Northants NN17 1TT

Printed and bound in Great Britain by
Biddles Ltd, Guildford and King's Lynn

British Library Cataloguing in Publication Data

Essential facts for managers.
 1. Management. Manuals
 I. British Institute of Management
 658.4

ISBN 1-85091-622-5

Contents

Introduction

In plain terms, this reference book is intended to ensure that managers know what they are talking about. Or, perhaps even more important, that they know what others are talking about.

It is not directed at any one particular management discipline. Coverage is of those subjects and areas common to management generally – the kind of subject that might easily crop up at any meeting with fellow managers or with clients or suppliers. The book is comprehensive where comprehensiveness is appropriate; concise when it isn't.

Essential facts for managers is for the working manager on his way up who suddenly finds he needs or wants to know more about a subject than he does. It helps him to know precisely what his accountant is talking about; it helps the accountant to know what the marketing manager means; it provides the common ground for all management.

Because it has been compiled for the working manager, there is no theorising, no academic conjecture. It is another step towards still better, practical management, thoughtfully compiled, meticulously researched, set out, of course, in plain terms.

1 Management techniques and theories

Action centred leadership

An action centred leadership course assumes that a manager has the technological competence to do his job and an adequate grasp of the technical aspects of management. It concentrates on developing a manager's ability to get the best out of those for whose work he is responsible and accountable.

Delegates to a course are given practical leadership exercises to perform while other delegates observe. At the end of an exercise the leader's performance is subjected to detailed evaluation, designed to bring out strengths and weaknesses.

Algorithms

As step by step procedures for finding a solution to a problem, algorithms are usually associated with computer programming but their use in various management functions is becoming more general. Although they may not be recognised as such, algorithms are already in common use in, for example, the instruction booklets accompanying domestic appliances such as washing machines. Most of these booklets include a trouble-finding guide which takes the form of naming the fault ('Machine will not start') and then lists the points to check ('Is the machine properly plugged in? Is the fuse blown? Are the electrical connections properly secured? Is the safety catch working properly?').

The questions are asked in a logical sequence: if, in the example, the machine is not properly plugged in the subsequent questions are irrelevant; and so on down the list.

Similar but rather more complicated algorithms are frequently used to reduce complex legislation to a form more easily understood by those it affects. A common adaptation in this context is in the construction of application forms for a particular purpose where there are a number of conditions to be fulfilled for the application to be successful. ('If you have answered "yes" to question 3, ignore questions 4, 5 and 6.')

In more general usage algorithms are usually presented as flow charts with arrows leading from one step to the next.

In the management context, construction of an algorithm can be helpful in any situation in which there are a number of definable steps and where each step has more than one possible consequence.

Assertiveness training

Both non-assertive and aggressive behaviour stem from a low level of self-esteem and both have undesirable effects on individuals and on their companies.

By developing a proper degree of assertiveness, as distinct from aggression, a manager will find his job more satisfying and he will do it better.

This basic concept requires a manager to develop his assertiveness by recognising the disagreeable consequence of non-assertive and aggressive behaviour. An example of non-assertive behaviour might be that of a manager who accepts extra work from a superior, knowing that he will not be able to do it in time. The manager may be motivated by a desire to please; unwillingness to appear obstructive; a belief that his career prospects will be affected by resistance. The consequences of his non-assertion may include shoddy performance of a job done in haste; resentment by his subordinates of the additional work he has undertaken for them to do; criticism for failing to stand up for them against senior management. Aggressive behaviour ('I can't possibly do that: I'm much too busy!') often draws an aggressive reaction ('That's your problem: get on with it.'). In subordinates, a persistently aggressive manager provokes non-assertive behaviour since they will avoid attracting aggression.

Assertive behaviour involves developing enough self-confidence to be able to put over a view in a civil, reasoned and firm way, without alienating colleagues.

Brainstorming

Brainstorming as a technique for producing ideas has been in use for some 50 years and during that period some clear guidelines for conducting a brainstorming session have emerged. These guidelines are based on the generally accepted concept that brainstorming is a means of getting a large number of ideas from a group of people in a short time.

The wording is chosen with care: the aim of a brainstorming session has to be to elicit any ideas, however frivolous or apparently impractical, and the success of a session is judged on the number of ideas produced. On the size of the group, the optimum number is usually regarded as 'about 12'. A short session is an essential ingredient for success: enthusiasm and creativity run out relatively quickly in a session. Given these conditions, the main guidelines for running a brainstorming session are:

- no idea advanced should be subjected to judgment at the session;
- no limits should be set on the range of ideas; participants should be encouraged to voice whatever notion might occur to them;
- emphasis must be on quantity, not quality, of ideas generated;
- cross-fertilisation, with one person developing another's idea, should be encouraged.

Given these basic guidelines, the conduct of a brainstorming session is seen as having six stages.
(1) The session needs just enough information from its leader about the

subject matter for which ideas are sought – but care is needed not to include data which might inhibit free-ranging creativity.

(2) Once the subject matter has been defined, the participants are then invited to re-state it in 'how to' terms. The purpose is to encourage participants to stand back from the subject matter and to re-state it in their own terms. A session invited to produce ideas for a new range of products could produce a re-statement response such as: 'what you are really asking is how to increase revenue.'

(3) Recommended practice is for the leader of the session to write down all the re-statements offered, prefacing them with 'in how many ways can we . . .' The leader then invites participants to choose which re-statement to take first: as ideas for each re-statement dry up he moves to the next.

(4) After the re-statement stage a warm-up session may be needed and the practice is for the leader to throw in any idea, however wild, and get participants to take it up. Examples might be: what would you do if you knew the world was going to end at 10.30 (BST) tonight? can you think of alternative uses for our ash trays?

(5) A warm-up session is taken as having achieved its objective when laughter is frequent and the ideas wild. The leader then takes the first re-statement chosen and invites ideas. As they are made, however wild, he writes them down, with a felt tipped pen, on a large sheet of paper. These sheets are torn off and displayed round the room.

(6) When the flow of ideas dries up, the leader selects what he considers to be the wildest of the wild ideas voiced and invites the session to turn it into something useful.

Business games

The novelty of business games, first developed in the 1950s, attracted early enthusiasm for them as a method of management training.

That enthusiasm appears to have waned a little. A volume of criticism has accumulated: delegates tend to see them as a game and play to win, not to learn; there is no effective way of evaluating them; they are expensive, if computer based; they create the illusion of reality; they ignore qualitative factors such as style, morale, labour relations.

However, business games are still used and it is said that their use will grow as management in general moves towards a more exact study, with a growing body of methodology. They are also finding a use as a means of advanced research into the probabilities that may arise from a particular business decision.

An increasingly common use of management games is in staff development programmes. A standard guide to management games, now in its third edition, is Chris Elgood's *Handbook of Management Games* published by Gower Publishing Company.

Critical path analysis

A major advantage of using critical path analysis (CPA) for planning purposes is that it imposes on management the discipline of developing a logical, properly thought-out approach to a project.

It can be used for any operation in which there is a recognisable beginning and end. It involves identifying each separate step in the project in logical sequence and allocating the time needed to complete each step. The process includes the time taken for the arrival of resources needed to complete each step.

A strength of CPA is that it represents the steps in a project in flow chart form. The beginning of each step is normally shown as a circle; the time taken to complete that step is represented by a line to the next step in the sequence. This visual presentation makes it easy to follow the critical path – the progress of the project and the time taken for its completion.

Critical path analysis is regarded as being particularly useful for major, one-off projects with at least some 100 or so stages. For very large operations CPA is normally done on computer.

Energy audit

There is no universal 'best buy' for energy. Each form has its advantages and disadvantages and technical requirements often dictate the selection of energy needed for a particular function. Any company may thus use a variety of fuels and a first requirement of an energy audit is to convert all energy consumed into a common unit — usually coal equivalent. The necessary conversion factors are listed in the table.

| | | | Equivalents | |
Fuel	Unit	Therms	Megajoules	Tonne of coal
Gas	I therm	I	105	0.0040
Electricity	I kWh	0.034	3.6	0.0005
Heating oil	I gallon	1.77	187	0.0074
Derv.	I gallon	1.62	171	0.0065
Petrol	I gallon	1.48	156	0.0058
Kerosine	I tonne	470	49600	1.70
Propane	I kg	0.47	49.6	0.0017
Coal	I tonne	261	27500	1.0

Effective energy audits are most commonly based on calculations of energy consumed in unit — not money — terms. Since fuel costs rise with inflation using money terms masks any energy savings resulting from an audit.

However, consideration of energy consumption in both money and unit terms provides a basis on which to take a view on what savings would be desirable. Depending on the view taken a company then has a choice over the size of an energy conservation programme appropriate to its position.

* Visual inspection of the energy using sites to determine what areas, if any, provide opportunities for energy saving.
* A systematic metering of all uses of energy, collection of all available data and relevant information.
* Development of a full scale energy conservation plan, based on data collected and possibly calling in professional advice.

The philosophy is that the cost of an energy audit should relate to the savings it produces.

Space heating

* Air curtains in doorways projecting air through nozzles at either ambient temperature or heated are efficient for preventing heat loss and are widely used.
* Individual oil or gas fired space heaters are usually more efficient than heaters served from a central source.
* Cleaning and recycling warm air within a building reduces the amount of heat wasted by extraction.
* Lightweight doors that close quickly are better draught preventers than any other.
* Radiant heating directed locally as required is usually more effective and cheaper than warm air heating, particularly for lofty buildings.
* Solar heating is not regarded as very suitable for general industrial use. In an average year, one square metre of solar panel is likely to collect up to 1,000 kWh.
* Radiators installed on uninsulated external walls can lose up to 10 per cent of heat output. Aluminium foil on the wall behind a radiator will virtually halt this loss.
* Signs of heat loss: wet roofs dry off quickly after rain; snow melts most quickly; birds congregate.
* Draughts are caused by differences in external and internal air pressures: identification of the causes of negative air pressure in a building can help reduce draughts.

Gantt charts

Gantt charts, originated early this century by engineer Henry Gantt as a graphic method of planning production times and quantities, are widely used and in a range of forms.

In essence, Gantt showed that if a company used its machinery to complete one order before starting on the next, production would be orderly but the machines would be under-utilised and completion times lengthened.

Gantt overlapped orders: he disregarded the sequence in which orders were accepted but adhered to the operation sequence each order specified.

A Gantt chart represents in the form of a rectangle the production time needed by a particular machine to complete a particular order. This visible presentation in graphic form makes it easy for a programme schedule to be juggled around to achieve maximum machine utilisation.

Gantt charts subsequently became the basis for critical path analysis and network planning methods in general.

Herzberg

Professor Frederick Herzberg (Case Western Reserve University, Cleveland, Ohio) identified two factors influencing work motivation: job content and job context. His research, in the late 1950s, demonstrated that jobs which people found most satisfying and motivating provided: opportunity for achievement; recognition; interesting, challenging work; responsibility and scope for advancement.

Jobs found to cause most dissatisfaction were those where company policy, human relationships, supervision, pay and working conditions were all seen as being poor or inadequate.

At first glance, Professor Herzberg's findings do not appear to be very surprising. Their usefulness is seen as being the clarity with which they focus attention on the motivational distinction between a job and the environment in which that job is performed. The inference of this distinction — that improving the environment in which a job is performed does not compensate for an unsatisfying job — has profoundly influenced thinking on the whole area of motivation.

Intrapreneurship

Intrapreneurship — entrepreneurship within a corporate entity — is a relatively new concept which is attracting increasing attention as a primary determinant of business success. Although intrapreneurship is new as a concept (it is thought it was first identified as such in 1976) it has been developing strongly over the past 20 years. Evidence of this is the growth of business start-ups in the United States and, to a lesser degree, in Britain. In the United States, it is estimated that, between 1970 and 1980, new business start-ups, led by ex-managers in

Gantt chart

Chart 1

	Monday	Tuesday	Wednesday	Thursday	Friday	Monday	Tuesday
Machine A	101			102	103	103	
Machine B		101			102		103
Machine C		101	102				

Chart 2

	Monday	Tuesday	Wednesday	Thursday	Friday
Machine A	101 104	102	105	103	
Machine B	105 101		102 103	104	103
Machine C	102	105 101	104		

Chart 1 shows jobs lined up in sequence as received. Chart 2 shows jobs rearranged (overlapped) for maximum machine loading.

corporate entities for the most part, created 20 million jobs. During the same period, numbers employed by the top US companies changed very little.

The view is that these figures show how executives, unable to persuade their company to back a new idea, increasingly tend to leave and start up on their own. For their part, companies are beginning to feel the need to take positive steps to encourage innovators to stay in their employ by backing their ideas.

In many companies new ideas come mostly from either the marketing or technical departments. But, wherever they come from, innovators are volunteers: born, not appointed. Since the failure rate is high, it is thought that any company pursuing a positive policy of encouraging new ideas from its staff should adopt perhaps three times as many as it may judge it needs to stay entrepreneurial.

Management by objectives

The concept of management by objectives was first formulated in the mid-1950s and was not always seen, at that time, as a major development in management technique. Many companies had for years been using the principles of management by objectives, at least in part and not necessarily under that name. It has since developed into a systematic management style which imposes on senior management a requirement for formulating an effective and practical corporate plan and on line managers a clear understanding of their role in achieving that plan plus a commitment to it.

In Britain, management by objectives tends to concentrate on corporate planning; in the United States the emphasis is on motivating the individual manager. Available research indicates that equal weight should be given to both.

In either case, it is generally accepted that effective management by objectives starts with the development of a corporate plan with line managers being involved in its creation. Individual objectives are arrived at by discussion with individual managers whose commitment to the plan and the objectives is critical.

Mentoring

Mentoring is a relative newcomer to management terminology but the concept it names has its origins in the old concept of apprenticeships. It involves spotting potential high-flyers at an early stage of career development and, in various ways, training and preparing them for promotion to higher office.

Selection of suitable candidates for mentoring can be both arbitrary and fortuitous if no formalised procedures for selection are drawn up by a particular company. However, with mentoring becoming steadily more commonplace in companies of all sizes, selection procedures (which usually involve a committee) are being developed to suit a company's needs.

The usual ingredients of selection procedures include: an annual assessment review; recommendations by department heads; regular reports on individual performance by department heads; a probing interview of all newcomers soon after they start work. In larger companies, it is commonplace for a senior manager to attend junior management meetings.

Selected candidates for mentoring are usually attached, formally or informally, to a senior manager who, it is thought, should be between 8 and 15 years older than his protégé. In many cases the candidate will share an office with his senior for a time during which he will undertake some of the senior's more routine work. It is not unusual for the senior to mould his protégé into his personal replacement on retirement.

It is believed that most companies have a mentoring programme of some kind even if they are not aware of it as a conscious process. Every corporate entity needs to have trained replacements ready to replace senior managements as they retire and for smaller companies internal mentoring provides a smooth handover. It has other benefits. It keeps senior management in closer touch with the workplace; it ensures that corporate strategies and philosophies are preserved.

For those not selected for mentorship an early awareness of their apparent lack of potential development in a particular company may be a spur to seek other possibilities. Or it may create an acceptance of the situation and a readiness to settle down to career development within the limits of their potential.

Motivation

The considerable research on motivation carried out since World War II has produced a number of theories but no total concept commonly applied in practice. Nevertheless, a substantial amount of research data is available and current thinking, spurred by the economic pressures of the 1980s, tends to centre round two distinct, but related sets of ideas. One concerns the factors, in a job, that motivate an individual; the other takes in the reasons why an individual behaves in a particular way in a particular job, including why he chose that job. On the factors motivating people, much research has been done on a theory that each individual has an hierarchy of needs:

- a job to earn a living;
- physical safety;
- the company of others;
- the esteem of colleagues and friends;
- growth potential.

According to this theory, each need — reading from the top — must be satisfied in turn before the remaining needs start to operate. Further, that once the first four of the needs listed are satisfied, they cease to operate as a source of motivation. The need to satisfy growth potential, however, remains. On the reasons for individual behaviour, a central theory is that motivation will be high when an individual's expectation of the outcome of doing a particular job is high.

Underlying these broad generalisations is a variety of theories, each tending to be slightly different from the others. There does, however, appear to be some findings which are common, to a greater or lesser extent, to many, perhaps most, of the ideas researched in the past decade or so.

- Motivation arises from a combination of factors, both in an individual himself and in the environment, physical and intellectual, in which he works.
- Although they may not be consciously aware of it, all individuals make positive decisions about the way they behave.
- Individuals have their own ambitions — which may be (and often are) quite modest — and goals which they want to achieve.
- Individuals do the things they think will lead to the results they want.
- Pay is an important factor in motivation, but job satisfaction can be equally important.

These factors add up to one very broad generalisation: an employee will do his job effectively when the rewards are those he values. It is not hard to see the force of this generalisation; however, applying it successfully in practice has not so far been anything like as easy.

It is widely accepted that tinkering with particular aspects of a job — job enrichment, merit payments — is not enough: the need is for a total concept in which a company has a rounded and integrated motivation policy.

The search for such a policy is a continuing process but some promising leads have emerged and are attracting interest. These leads follow realisation that motivation levels are very high among the top executives of a company. They are central to the company's activities and have a sense of entrepreneurship and enterprise which is not shared by the rest of the organisation. With the intention of sharing this sense of enterprise down the organisational ladder, some large companies have begun to create autonomous, smaller plants with each being a separate and distinct profit centre within the total organisation. Rewards in the smaller plants are related to performance; employees are encouraged to feel they are doing a valuable job contributing clearly to performance and they are kept informed of the plant's progress.

An adaptation of this decentralising process is the creation of small work groups within a single organisation, with each group responsible for a particular area of the company's operation in a highly autonomous way.

Experience with these developments suggests that there are a number of factors which produce reactions in a work force favourable to a high level of motivation:

- a link between pay and the operating results of the employing organisation;
- a positive policy of keeping employees regularly and fully informed on results;
- making sure that employees in a pay-results policy company understand how the scheme works;
- making no distinction between employees, such as separate rest rooms for senior employees, special car parking facilities, time clocks for junior workers;
- creation of a plant committee to contribute towards management decisions;
- breaking down operations into small work units, each with an agreed goal to achieve.

Negotiating

Running through all the considerable research available on negotiating techniques is one overall principle: conduct the negotiating as if the other side is going to be your public relations agent. This, it is said, is because that is precisely what will happen; the other side will circulate *their* perception of the way you have gone about things, not yours.

Such an approach is not intended to exclude the use of any negotiating tactics appropriate to a particular situation. It recognises that a successful negotiation is one in which both sides believe they have won or, at least, that a fair compromise has been achieved.

It also recognises that in any negotiation — ranging from a salesman selling a product to a super power summit meeting — the fact that negotiating is taking place means that both sides want to come to an agreement. A starting point, therefore, has to be the collection of relevant information on the subject matter of the negotiation; determining both whether and on what to negotiate; a clear understanding of the other side's position, point of view and room to manoeuvre.

Available research discourages attempts to win some psychological advantages such as negotiating on home ground, attempts to impose deadlines, and take-it-or-leave-it proposals. The other side, if it has done its preliminary work, will recognise the tactics and be irritated by them, not impressed. The most commonly recommended first approach is to seek to establish common ground. This is easier when both sides are willing, for tactical reasons, to make known the whole of their requirements at once. The alternative — making known requirements one by one where the issues under negotiation are complex — requires more patience but a search for common ground for each step remains a recommended guiding principle.

Some other general principles thrown up by research are:

- know what you want and don't worry about what others get;
- be frank, honest and firm;
- volunteer answers to questions that the other side have not asked;
- once agreement is reached, settle: don't press for minor concessions.

PERT

PERT, acronym for programme evaluation and review technique, is a simple and easily applied method of assessing probabilities. It is often used for forecasting future sales revenue but it was originally developed to calculate the time likely to take to complete a production process. It is particularly useful in situations where managements have no previous experience of a particular project.

The PERT method requires that each self-contained stage in a production process is identified. Three views are then taken on the time needed to complete each stage: optimistic, pessimistic and most likely. These three estimates are submitted to a simple formula to determine the expected time:

$$\text{Expected time} = \frac{\text{Optimistic time} + \text{pessimistic time} + 4 \times \text{most likely time}}{6}$$

To take, as an example, the time for hanging a picture:

Optimistic: 2 minutes (no problems)
Pessimistic: 10 minutes (wall is hard; hammer hits thumb; nail bends)
Most likely: 3 minutes

The formula gives this outcome for the expected time:

$$4 \text{ mins} = \frac{2 + 10 + 12}{6}$$

Such a calculation may well be enough for many estimating purposes. A refinement which is often used is to apply a standard variation to the expected time as calculated above to provide a likely margin of error on each side of it. The standard variation is calculated by subtracting the optimistic time from the pessimistic time and dividing the result by six. This would give a standard variation of $1\frac{1}{3}$ in the above example.

Certain rules are commonly observed in making the estimates on which the PERT technique is based.

- They must not be influenced by any known deadlines.
- Each stage must be considered independently of any other. Hanging a picture in the above example assumes the picture, string, nails and hammer have all been delivered. The delivery stage would be an independent factor.

- The various stages must be assessed in a random, not logical, sequence.
- It must be made clear to those providing the figures that they are estimates and not schedules to which they will subsequently be committed.
- Extreme possibilities should not be included in the estimates. The picture hanging estimates, for example, should not include the possibility of dropping the picture, breaking the glass and of having to have it re-framed. It might, however, include the possibility of having to tighten the string; or of having to use a Rawl plug and screw rather than a nail.

The Peter Principle

The Peter Principle is that in any hierarchy every employee tends to rise to his level of incompetence. The principle was presented by L F Peter in his book *The Peter Principle* published in 1969.

A starting point in developing his principle came when he sent off application forms properly filled in and his cv for a teaching job. He had them returned with a letter saying they could not be accepted unless they have been registered at a Post Office to ensure safe delivery. Mr Peter commented: 'As I looked further afield, I found that every organisation contained a number of persons who could not do their jobs.'

His book is a wry exposé of the tendency to believe that an employee who is competent in one job will also be competent in a more senior job. A consequence of this is a further principle which Mr Peter states as: in time every post tends to be occupied by an employee who is incompetent to carry out his duties. From which it follows, he argues: work is accomplished by those employees who have not yet reached their level of incompetence.

Product life cycle

The concept that every product has a life cycle taking it through several stages and, eventually, into decline, is well documented, but not always widely used in practice. Nevertheless, application of the life cycle concept, suitably adapted to a particular company's business can play a useful role in helping to form long-term marketing strategies. The concept detects five stages in a product's useful life.

Introduction

The failure rate for launching a new product is high. If, however, a new product is sufficiently new and sufficiently well-marketed to establish that a sizeable demand exists for it, its sales will, after varying periods, according to product, begin to grow. In the introductory period, sales will be slow to rise: the rate will subsequently increase.

Growth

It is not always easy to determine when a product moves from the introductory to the growth stage. Most of the sales in the introductory stage come as a result of gaining customer awareness and setting up effective distribution channels. This stage merges imperceptibly into growth when repeat orders build up, competitors start eyeing the market, new distribution channels open up and the sales revenue curve begins to move sharply higher.

The growth period is often the most lucrative of a product's life. Its length can be short and a product with obvious and immediate advantages for the consumer can jump from introduction to growth very quickly. For others, requiring a change in existing consumer habits — the introduction of instant coffee to a tea drinking nation — growth can cover many years.

Maturity

During the growth stage, competitors will have entered the market and their marketing activities will have helped to spread product awareness.

Other, competing new products may have emerged. Fashions may have changed. The market then enters into maturity when expansion has slowed and when the only new business available is that taken from competitors. Maturity often exists for very many years: vacuum cleaners, sewing machines, Rolls Royce cars and umbrellas, for example, have been in the market for very many years and show no signs of going into decline. Other products, such as skateboards, frisbees and stiletto heels, tend not to last too long.

Saturation

In turn, maturity produces a situation in which too many companies enter the market, price wars break out and, with no market growth likely, businesses drop out of the market. It is during this period that the sales curve starts turning downwards. If nothing happens to arrest the downturn, the market goes into decline.

Decline

Withdrawal from the market is not always the wisest move when it enters a decline, although, for most companies, it is. If a company finds that its share of a declining market is rising because others are getting out it may be worth-while staying in the business, without devoting any significant marketing budget to it.

The product life cycle concept requires that a company should know the phase a product is in before entering the market with a competing product of its own. The growth period is clearly the one to aim for in most cases. The concept also requires that a company is ready with a new product when it realises that maturity is giving way to decline. American car manufacturers, for example, come up with a new model every five years.

The product life cycle concept is itself demonstrating the characteristics it identifies. A newer variation suggests that, mainly for consumer products, a cycle can show staircase patterns. A commonly quoted example is that of nylon which, for most people, is thought of as starting life as stockings and parachutes but is now used for a very wide range of products including fishing lines and carpets. Each new product-use boosted sales.

Project appraisal

Project appraisal involves the consideration of three fundamental factors: pro-fitability; the time value of money: future cash flows. Four widely recognised methods of appraisal, taking account of these factors to varying degrees, are commonly used. They are: (a) accounting rate of return; (b) payback; (c) net present value; and (d) internal rate of return.

Accounting rate of return

In its simplest terms, the accounting rate of return (also known as return on capital employed) is arrived at by dividing the anticipated profit by the capital required to produce it: this is calculated for the expected life of the project, year by year. Mostly, the period taken is the first five years of the project's life. The method is simple to use since it is based on easily understood and widely used accounting procedures. But it does not take into account the different timing of cash flows arising from a project with a life of some years.

Payback

Payback is the number of years from the start of a project before the initial cash outflow is recovered from the cash inflows arising from the project. It is simple to apply but it ignores cash flows subsequent to the payback period. Nevertheless it is a widely used method particularly in an industry which is subject to rapid technological change. It also serves as a backup for other project appraisal methods: the further away the recovery of capital, the more uncertain it is that the capital will, in fact, be recovered.

Net present value

The method requires a decision on the minimum return (after payment of tax) acceptable to a company from a particular project. It then applies this rate of return to the cash flows expected to arise from the project for each year of its anticipated working life (or, often as not, for its first five years).

The result is a figure, allowing for inflation, which shows the net present value of money to be received over a period of years. The net present value method is often used and, theoretically, is the most acceptable. But it has three potential drawbacks.

- It does not take into account the size of a project. Two projects may have the same net present value but one may need a much higher level of initial investment.
- Because the net present value method does not indicate a return on capital invested it makes it more difficult to assess the risk involved.
- It relies on agreement on the rate of return acceptable to a company: furthermore, application of the rate is a complex accounting process.

For these reasons, there is a tendency to avoid use of the net present value method in favour of the internal rate of return method.

Internal rate of return

The method in its simplest form provides the percentage earned on the capital invested in each year of the life of the project after allowing for repayment of the sum originally invested. The process involved is complicated: it involves repeated calculations of the net present value of cash flows using different rates of return until the net present value is as near to zero as possible. Once the internal rate of return has been determined, it can be compared with a required target rate of return to determine whether the project is financially acceptable.

None of the four methods can take into account the commercial considerations involved in a project: they are each purely concerned with measuring the returns to the company, making certain assumptions which experience may or may not justify. Nevertheless, as aids to management decision, they can be very important.

Purchasing management

Purchasing was one of the last management functions to be delegated to a specialist. It is perhaps because purchasing management is relatively new that it is said that the importance of material costs is not always as widely recognised as it should be. American experience is that, as a broad generalisation, material costs can take up a little over 50 per cent of a company's sales revenues. On this broad base, it is argued that a two per cent change in material costs could produce a change of between 10–12 per cent in bottom line profits.

Similar calculations have been applied to UK experience. One published estimate is that in a manufacturing company with a turnover of £50–100 million a one per cent cut in material costs would produce the same impact on gross profits as a four per cent reduction in direct labour costs.

However, precise identification of material costs for many companies is not a simple process. Inflation can mask movements in costs from one year to another; with perhaps many thousands of items involved, keeping track of cost is a sizeable problem; quality and smooth delivery are as important, often as not, as cost; a purchasing manager's quest for big discounts on quantity may conflict with stock control policies.

It is estimated that 40 per cent of all purchase orders made by companies are for less than £50 in value. The simple act of placing an order can be costly: further, some suppliers, reluctant to undertake the administration involved, make a minimum charge for small orders.

It follows that it makes sense to keep large stocks of those items on which relatively small amounts of money are spent each year.

Strategic management

Published research results support the belief that companies that implement strategic management outperform those who do not. Long range planning, including the construction in advance of alternative courses of action to meet external changes, is now widely regarded as an essential requirement for general management.

The very substantial literature on strategic management offers a variety of approaches but is unanimous in the importance it attaches to the first step: establishing a company's strategic objectives over a period, often five years. The process involves a large number of factors and is likely to be a very fundamental one. A specialist publishing company, for example, might, as a result of an appraisal process, decide that it is really in the business of selling information and extend its activities to computerised information systems.

Stock control

The total value of all stocks held by UK business organisations is estimated to be around 25 per cent of the country's gross domestic output. In the United

States, the costs of holding stock, expressed as a percentage of the cost of goods sold, range from 65 per cent in manufacturing to 93 per cent in wholesaling.

Cost-effective control of stocks is, therefore, a major function of management. Three ratios are used to measure a company's performance in the area of stock control:

Return on assets employed

$$\frac{\text{Profit}}{\text{Total assets}} \times 100$$

The higher the ratio, the more effective the use of assets

Current ratio

$$\frac{\text{Current assets}}{\text{Current liabilities}} \times 100$$

The ratio is a measure of liquidity and provides an indication of the use of working capital to maintain stocks

$$\frac{\text{Cost of sales}}{\text{Average stock}} \times 100$$

A more direct ratio, for stock control purposes: the higher the ratio, the better the use of stock.

Control of stock is linked directly with the control of production. But since management cannot control the level of sales or the delivery time of supplies, a company must keep stocks as a buffer between supply and demand.

This is the main reason for holding stock but a manufacturing company may have to hold a number of different kinds of stock: raw materials (for making its products); work-in-progress (partly made-up items); finished goods; spares for the production machinery; general items (stationery, cleaning materials); stocks of material for testing and inspection.

One much-used method contributing towards the efficient control of stock involves calculation of the annual requirement value for each item held in stock. It is arrived at by multiplying the unit value (cost) of the item by the number of times it is used each year. The resulting table of annual replacement values shows up which items need the closest attention, in stock control terms.

It is a common experience to find that around 20 per cent of the items account for 80 per cent of the total annual requirement value. This effect is known as either the 20/80 rule or, when expressed in graph form, as the Pareto curve — named after an Italian sociologist, Vilfredo Pareto, who observed that there is an inverse relationship between the percentages of items in a set of items and their importance.

Of the various stock control methods used by companies in varying areas of activity, three are basic:

- *Fixed re-order interval*
  Orders of varying sizes are placed at fixed intervals (weekly, monthly etc) to keep stocks at a pre-determined level.
- *Fixed re-order level*
  Orders are placed at varying intervals to maintain a pre-determined level.
- *Two-bin system*
  Often used for stocking small items. Stock of an item is held in two separate containers; a replacement order is placed when one bin is emptied.

Stress

American research into managerial stress accepts that it is (a) part of the job, (b) not necessarily harmful and (c) lists a number of techniques for coping with job tension. At the top of the American list is: regular sleep and exercise.

However, the research also indicates that insomnia is one of the major symptoms of stress so alternative techniques are listed as: regular physical exercise to help induce sleep; a clear separation of work from non-work activities; discussion with colleagues at the place of work; withdrawal from a situation identified as producing the stress.

Although the importance of recognising stress and of dealing with it is widely accepted there seems also to be a general view that most managers know instinctively how to cope. It is when stress begins to show physical, recognisable symptoms — insomnia, undue irritability, heavy drinking — that instinctive reaction may be inadequate. The psychology of stress sees it as being a result of either fear of some external and unknown factor; anxiety over some known, internal factor; and guilt, said to be first cousin of anxiety. Any one or combination of these factors may produce a general emotional discomfort broadly expressed as a feeling of inability to cope properly with the day's work. This view of stress believes that every individual has an image of what he would like to be or achieve and another image of his current self. The greater the difference between the two images, it is said, the greater the lack of self-esteem and the greater the proneness to undue stress.

T groups

T-group training is based on group therapy methods used in psychiatry and has attracted both enthusiasm and suspicion since it was first developed as a management development technique in the United States in the late 1940s.

The technique requires that a T (training) group should meet away from its place of work; that there should be no planned agenda; that there should be no leader. There must, however, be one trainer whose function is to spark off and maintain discussion — but not to influence the group in any particular direction. Experience in Britain suggests an optimum group size of 7–10; in America groups of up to 16 are not uncommon.

Although the purposes of setting up a particular T group may vary slightly, they most commonly aim to:

- sharpen awareness of how others react to one's own behaviour;
- increase perception of relationships between others;
- develop an ability to react effectively to any changes required as a result of these two factors.

In a typical first session of a T group, the trainer will explain the aims of the group and list meeting times. He may indicate his willingness to help, but not say how. The group is thus in a vacuum, with no agenda, no hierarchy and no chairman.

The basic concept behind the technique is that this vacuum can be, and mostly is, disturbing: a consequence is that individual members are forced to re-examine the process of working with groups and/or of influencing other people.

There appears to be no commonly accepted view on the effectiveness of T groups as a means of developing management skills in the important area of dealing with people. This is likely to be because of the difficulty of measuring the results of a particular group. American experience is that T-group training has been shown to have overcome management versus employees feelings in many companies. Another American experience is that the introduction of specific management problems into a T-group agenda has worked well.

Transactional analysis

As a means of heightening an individual's ability to relate well with others, the effectiveness of transactional analysis has yet to be established. Regarded as a rather shallow theory of human behaviour it has not so far attracted a strong base in research.

The theory is that each individual behaves, at various times, as a parent, child or adult. An example of the three patterns would be the response to a request by a colleague for a particular file.

Parent: 'I'll get it for you and put it on your desk.'
Child: 'I'm too busy with my own problems'.
Adult: 'It's in the blue filing cabinet'.

By recognising these patterns and observing the reaction of others the transactional analysis theory suggests that behaviour can be adjusted to create improved general relationships.

Zero-based budgeting

Zero-based budgeting is a relatively new management technique (it first emerged, in the United States, in the early 1960s) and is probably one of the most difficult to apply successfully. It is called zero-based because each manager in a business organisation is required to start with a blank sheet of paper — zero base. He is then required to determine the objectives of his function — and to have those objectives agreed and approved by top management. The next step is to list alternative ways of achieving the agreed objectives — and to make as certain as he can that nothing has been left out.

A decision is then needed on the best alternative for achieving the desired objectives. This involves calculation of various costs for the various alternatives as well as the general practicabilities involved. Thereafter, the manager has to break down the preferred alternative into tactical steps and assess the costs and benefits of each step. Finally, he must outline what could happen if his overall proposal is rejected. The burden of proving the commercial viability to his company of his chosen course of action rests with the manager: top management has to be convinced by the weight of argument.

Evaluation of each manager's proposal is the final, vital step in top management's tactics for converting their long-range planning into a final budget and operating plan. Zero-based budgeting integrates planning, budgeting and decision making; equally important, it involves an aggressive search for alternative ways of doing things. Its successful application requires commitment from all the managers concerned, based on a clear understanding of the company's long-term strategies and their endorsement of them.

2 Sales and marketing

Essential Facts for Managers

Advertising

For most companies, it is not usually possible to measure precisely the cost-effectiveness of a particular advertising campaign, irrespective of its size. Movements in sales revenue following a campaign may offer some general indications, but sales figures are subject to the behaviour of a number of factors of which advertising may be only one. Comparing movements in revenue after one campaign with those obtained after another may help, but such comparisons can mask the impact of change in the market place in the intervening period.

A marketing manager contemplating an advertising campaign has, first, a choice of media: the press; television; radio; posters. Each of these media will be able to provide a breakdown of readership, viewers or listeners. He has, too, to be clear on what his advertising is intended to achieve. Advertising can be used: to create awareness of a new product; to inform; to attract enquiries which, it is hoped, will lead to orders; to create an image for the company or its products; to reach buying personnel in potential client companies who would otherwise be inaccessible to a sales force; to achieve direct sales — through including a return order coupon on the advertisement; to defend a company's products against competition; to retain customer loyalty.

Underlying these choices is the paramount need to know who a company's customers are and to know something about their wants, perceived and actual. It is usual to divide customers into two main categories: those who buy products and services rationally: they weigh the cost against the usefulness to them of the product; those whose buying decision is influenced by other than purely rational considerations — the implied prestige of owning an expensive product; prevailing environmental and cultural patterns; aspirations; family influence and so on.

Benefit segregation

This division is interesting, but not particularly helpful to a marketing manager. It is usual, for practical purposes, to define customer behaviour by what has become known as benefit segregation. This divides customers into those who buy a product for its functional characteristics; because it is relatively cheap; for its ready availability in, say, local supermarkets; for emotional reasons (a gift for a wife/husband); or for a combination of any of these reasons.

This breakdown provides a reasonable basis for further decisions on which media to employ. For consumer markets, the grouping most usually employed is a breakdown of social status as measured by jobs. The higher categories are usually light television viewers but form the principal readership of particular daily or specialised publications.

Looming behind all these factors is the common phenomenon, known as the Pareto effect, which observes that for virtually every company a small proportion of customers account for a large proportion of their business. This is often called the 20/80 rule whereby about 20 per cent of customers account for 80 per cent of business. The successful identification of the 20 per cent can be the most vital factor in achieving cost-effective advertising.

Changing styles

Influenced partly by new legislation and partly by changes in the general economic, political and cultural climate, the style of advertising has changed considerably over the past 10 years. One result of consumer protection legislation has been a distinct leaning towards rather bland advertisements that concentrate more on image building than hard selling based on claims. There can be few people in Britain who do not know the name of a beer that reaches parts that others cannot. Television commercials have become entertaining in themselves, often using a touch of light humour to put over a product image.

Philosophies

Various overall advertising philosophies are available for consideration:

- Advertising should develop a unique selling proposition (USP) for a product or product range and use it over a continuing period.
- Advertising directed at women should feature women or babies, or both: for men, use men.
- Advertisements should never under-estimate the intelligence of the consumer, or over-estimate his knowledge.
- Advertising featuring a girl in a bikini attracts attention — to the girl.
- Big advertisements create confidence.
- Advertising is not a science but an art and art knows no rules.

Excavation at Pompeii, the Roman city overwhelmed by an eruption of Vesuvius almost 20 centuries ago, disclosed a number of advertisements on the walls of buildings. One, on the wall of an inn, showed a centurion saying: 'I always drink Falernian wine.' The short list of philosophies listed above suggests: (a) the media was right; (b) using a man was right; (c) the slogan was clear, direct and unmistakable. That was right, too.

Radio and TV advertising

The 1981 Broadcasting Act imposes on the Independent Broadcasting Authority (IBA) an obligation to draw up a code governing standards and practice in broadcast advertising: and to ensure the code is complied with.

The code itself has some 37 rules and three detailed appendices dealing with advertising and children, financial advertising, the advertising of medicines and statutes affecting broadcast advertising. A selection of the more important rules is listed below.

- The general principle which will govern all broadcast advertising is that it should be legal, decent, honest and truthful. It is recognised that this principle is not peculiar to broadcasting, but is one which applies to all reputable advertising in other media in this country. Nevertheless, broadcasting, and particularly television, because of its greater intimacy within the home, gives rise to problems which do not necessarily occur in other media and it is essential to maintain a consistently high quality of broadcast advertising.
- Advertisements must comply in every respect with the law, common or statute.
- The detailed rules set out below are intended to be applied in the spirit as well as the letter and should be taken as laying down the minimum standards to be observed.
- The word 'advertisement' has the meaning implicit in the Broadcasting Act 1981, i.e. any item of publicity inserted in the programmes broadcast by the Authority in consideration of payment to a programme contractor or to the Authority.
- No advertisement may include anything that states, suggests, or implies, or could reasonably be taken to state, suggest or imply, that any part of any programme broadcast by the Authority has been supplied or suggested by any advertiser.
- Any advertisement must be clearly distinguishable as such and recognisably separate from the programmes. In particular:
  (a) situations and performances reminiscent of programmes must not be used in such a way as to blur the distinction between programmes and advertisements. In marginal cases the acceptance of an advertisement having such themes may depend upon some positive introductory indication that this is an advertiser's announcement.
  (b) the expression 'News Flash' must not be used as an introduction to an advertisement, even if preceded by an advertiser's name.
- The rules do not prohibit the inclusion of an advertisement by reason only of the fact that it is related in subject matter to an adjacent programme – e.g. advertisements for farm products and fertilisers in intervals around a farming programme. It is also acceptable for an advertisement to announce the direct and significant contribution of an advertiser's products to performances in events that have been broadcast – e.g. motor races or rallies. Normally, however, no reference to a programme is acceptable in an advertisement.

Printed advertising

Print advertising has its own system of self-regulation administered by the Advertising Standards Authority (ASA). The ASA produces and constantly reviews (a) the British Code of Advertising Practice (currently in its seventh edition) and (b) British Code of Sales Promotion Practice (now in its fourth edition).

The philosophy behind the British Code of Advertising Practice is set out in the three principles which are termed the essence of good advertising:

- all advertisements should be legal, decent, honest and truthful;
- all advertisements should be prepared with a sense of responsibility, both to the consumer and to society;
- all advertisements should conform to the principles of fair competition as generally accepted in business.

The code operates on the basis of the following rules:

Legality:

- Advertisements should contain nothing which is in breach of the law, nor omit anything which the law requires.
- Advertisements should contain nothing which is likely to bring the law into disrepute.

Decency:

- Advertisements should contain nothing which, because of its failure to respect the standards of decency and propriety that are generally accepted in the UK, is likely to cause either grave or widespread offence.
- Some advertisements, which do not conflict with the preceding sub-paragraph, may nonetheless be found distasteful because they reflect or give expression to attitudes or opinions about which society is divided. Where this is the case, advertisers are urged to consider the effect any apparent disregard of such sensitivities may have upon their reputation and that of their product; and upon the acceptability, and hence usefulness, of advertising generally.
- The fact that a product may be found offensive by some people is not, in itself, a sufficient basis under the code for objecting to an advertisement for it. Advertisers are urged, however, to avoid unnecessary offence when they advertise any product which may reasonably be expected to be found objectionable by a significant number of those who are likely to see their advertisement.

Honesty:

- No advertiser should seek to take improper advantage of any characteristic or circumstance which may make consumers vulnerable; as, for example, by exploiting their credulity or their lack of experience or knowledge in any manner detrimental to their interests.
- The design and presentation of advertisements should be such as to allow

each part of the advertiser's case to be easily grasped and clearly understood.

Truthful presentation (General):

• No advertisement, whether by inaccuracy, ambiguity, exaggeration, omission or otherwise, should mislead consumers about any matter likely to influence their attitude to the advertised product.

Specific rules deal with the application of these principles to particular situations. There are detailed rules for specialised areas as follows:

Health Claims
Hair and Scalp
Vitamins and Minerals
Slimming
Cosmetics
Mail Order

Financial Advertising
Employment and Business
   Opportunities
Limited Editions
Children

Sales promotion

Some of the basic principles of the code are listed below.

• Legality: all sales promotions should be legal. The code is designed to complement legal controls, not to usurp, or replace them.
• Spirit of the code: the code is to be applied in the spirit as well as in the letter with the aim of eliminating practices which might lead sales promotion into disrepute.
• Fair competition: all sales promotions should adhere to the principles of fair competition as generally accepted in business.
• Consumer interest: all sales promotions should deal fairly and honourably with consumers and should be seen to do so. No promoter, or other person engaged in the conduct of a sales promotion, should abuse the trust of consumers or exploit their lack of experience or knowledge to their detriment.
• Consumer satisfaction: sales promotions should be so designed and conducted as not to cause avoidable disappointment.
• Fairness: the terms and conduct of promotions should be equitable to all who are affected by them.
• The public interest: neither the design nor the conduct of a promotion should be such as to conflict with the public interest. In particular, promotions should contain nothing which is likely to provoke, or may appear to condone, violent or anti-social behaviour, damage to property or the causing of nuisance or injury to any member of the public.
• Truthful presentation: the presentation of a promotion should be clear and honest and should not be likely to mislead those who are addressed, or those to whose attention such material is likely to come.

- Limitations: any factor which is likely to affect a decision whether or not to participate in a promotion should be communicated in such a way that the consumer can take into account before being committed to any purchase which may be necessary for participation.
- Suitability of promotion to those reached by it: promoters should take all reasonable steps to ensure that neither advertising nor promotional material reaches those for whom the promotion concerned may be inappropriate.
- Administration: the administration should be prompt and efficient, so that consumers are given no grounds for justified complaint.

Agency agreements

Agency agreements are normally seen as straightforward arrangements whereby one party, the principal, authorises another, the agent, to act on his behalf in a particular set of circumstances. However, the law makes it possible for an agency to be presumed to exist if the conduct of the principal gives the impression that an agency has been created. The most obvious example of such a presumption is that a wife is deemed to have the authority to pledge her husband's credit for the purchase of necessities.

The law goes further: a third party dealing with an agent within a particular business area may reasonably assume that the agent has the degree of authority to act which is normal in that business. Thus, if an agent's authority is restricted in some way by the principal that restriction is no defence in law if a third party did not know of the restriction and if, in normal circumstances, it would be reasonable to assume that no such restriction existed. Take, for example, the case of the manager of a public house whose principal restricts his purchasing authority to buying beers and mineral waters: all other items are supplied by the principal. The manager's name is over the pub door as licensee. The manager, noting a demand from his customers, buys a particular brand of cigars from a manufacturer. Because public house managers might reasonably be expected to buy cigars and because the manager's name was displayed as licensee, a court would almost certainly uphold the cigar manufacturer's claim for payment if the principal refused to pay on the grounds that the manager was exceeding his authority.

But the concept of 'normal and reasonable in the circumstances' has some pitfalls. The essence of an agency agreement involving an agent in buying materials for a principal is that the agent must buy as cheaply as he can. A broker of a particular commodity might well follow a trade custom of buying in bulk to satisfy the requirements of a number of principals. The broker might then be seen as a seller, not as an agent: his principal might refuse to pay and might be successful in a court action if he could establish that he could have bought the goods more cheaply elsewhere. The fact that the broker acted normally and reasonably in the circumstances of his trade would not necessarily be seen as adequate defence.

Brand management

For a company with a mix of products, division of those products into brand groupings and placing each group under the direction of a brand manager, is an effective and practical marketing strategy. This approach reflects the fact that each product has its own characteristics and needs its own marketing plan. A brand manager's responsibility is usually to:

- collect and analyse all available market data concerning the product(s) for which he is responsible;
- produce a marketing plan which will achieve the objectives outlined by senior management;
- co-ordinate the activities of the departments that may be involved with the product or service so as to put the plan into practice;
- constantly review progress and be ready to introduce adjustments to the overall plan as changes in the market occur.

Although effective brand management requires considerable skill and experience it is not regarded as a specific marketing concept. It is a practical way for a marketing director to delegate responsibility.

Competition

The Director General of Fair Trading is empowered (by the Competition Act, 1980) to investigate any business practice which has, or is intended or likely to have the effect of restricting, distorting or preventing competition.

The test of whether a practice is anti-competitive is based on its effect, not its form.

Factors which the Director General may examine in considering whether to investigate particular practices may include:

- the market position of the company concerned and its market power, whether on a local or a national level;
- the relevant market in which competition might be affected. The effects of the practice may influence competition at several different levels and may have effects outside the company's main market;
- the company's intentions — it is not necessary for a practice actually to have an anti-competitive effect; it is sufficient for it to be intended to have, or be likely to have, such an effect.

The relevant legislation does not provide much guidance on what is regarded as anti-competitive practice but practices which might be anti-competitive include the following.

Pricing

- *Price discrimination* — the practice of selling goods or services to distinct and separate customers or groups of customers at different prices when the price differences do not reflect the differences in costs of supplying those customers. Price discrimination often takes the form of differential discounting or rebates from list prices and can artificially enhance the ability of a powerful buyer to compete on price in the market in which he is selling. Discriminatory prices may also be charged to a particular customer or group of customers or in a particular area in order to prevent or threaten competition in a segment of a supplier's market;
- *Predatory pricing* — the practice of temporarily selling below cost, with the intention of eliminating competition, so that in the future prices may be raised and enhanced profits achieved;
- *Vertical price squeezing* — when a vertically integrated company controls the total supply of an input which is essential to the production requirements of its subsidiary and its competitors. The input price can be raised and the final output price reduced, so that the profits of competitors are squeezed.

Distribution

- *Tie-in sales* — where a buyer must purchase part or all of his requirements of a second (tied) product from the supplier of a first (tying) product;
- *Full-line forcing* — where a buyer must purchase quantities of each item in a product range in order to be able to buy any of them;
- *Rental-only contracts* — where a customer is restricted to rental or lease terms where there are no alternative methods of acquiring the goods in question;
- *Exclusive supply* — where a seller supplies only one buyer in a certain geographical area;
- *Exclusive purchase* — where a buyer agrees to purchase or stock only the products of one manufacturer (possibly in return for an exclusive supply arrangement);
- *Selective distribution* — where sales outlets are chosen on a discriminatory basis.

Refusal to deal

These and other anti-competitive policies may be supported by a refusal to deal with those who do not meet certain requirements; for example minimum price levels may be established by a refusal to supply discounters. The refusal to deal may itself be an anti-competitive practice.

If, following investigation by the Director General of Fair Trading a case is referred to the Monopolies and Mergers Commission, the Commission must investigate:

- whether, at any time in the 12 months prior to the reference, any company mentioned in the reference was following, in relation to the goods or services specified, the named course of conduct or any course of conduct which appears to the Commission to be similar in form and effect;
- whether, by following such a course of conduct, the person was during that period engaged in an anti-competitive practice; and
- if the practice was anti-competitive, whether it operated, or might be expected to operate, against the public interest.

Public interest

In deciding whether a practice is, or could be, against the public interest, the Commission are required to take into account all relevant matters but in particular to have regard to the desirability of:

- maintaining and promoting effective competition in the supply of goods and services in the UK;
- promoting the interests of consumers, purchasers and users of goods and services in the UK in respect of prices, quality, and variety;
- promoting the reduction of costs, the development and use of new techniques and new products, and the entry of new competitors;
- maintaining and promoting a balanced distribution of industry and employment in the UK; and
- maintaining and promoting competitive activity in the markets outside the UK on the part of UK producers of goods and suppliers of goods and services.

Competition in the EEC

The consequences of infringing the European Community's competition rules range from massive fines (10 per cent of the offending company's or group's turnover) to the costs of dismantling unacceptable trading arrangements. Prohibited practices include:

(a) the direct or indirect fixing of purchase or selling prices;
(b) the direct or indirect fixing of any other trading conditions (including retail price maintenance by manufacturers);
(c) limitation or control of production, markets, technical development or investment*;

(d)   market sharing;
(e)   sharing sources of supply;
(f)   discrimination between one customer and another in similar transactions;
(g)   subjecting a contract to the acceptance of additional obligations which, in ordinary commercial practice, have no connection with the contract itself.

*Limiting production or eliminating normal market competitiveness can, in the Commission's view, be achieved by sharing information.

Consumer protection legislation

Consumer protection legislation imposes on the suppliers of goods and services considerable requirements all designed to protect the consumer (as distinct from a commercial customer) and all in addition to the requirements normally implied by contract law. The legislation is embodied in three main Acts: Trade Description Acts 1968–1972; Fair Trading Act 1973 and Consumer Credit Act 1974.

Trade Description Acts

The Acts make it an offence for any person who, in the normal course of trading, applies a false description to any goods or services with the intention of inducing a potential consumer to place an order. The Acts do not apply to private transactions and the false statement must be regarded as misleading to a serious degree.

On the supply of goods, the Acts apply to a trader both as a prospective seller and as a prospective buyer. For example, an antique dealer who pays a private person a nominal sum for an item of furniture, claiming that it is of no particular value, and who later sells it at a substantial profit could be liable to prosecution.

They also apply to a retailer who sells goods for which false claims have been made by the manufacturer or his agent. False or misleading indications as to price are also caught by the Acts:

- it is an offence for a supplier of goods to indicate, falsely, that the goods are being offered at a price less than either the manufacturers' recommended retail price or a price lower than previously offered by the supplier: this particularly affects goods offered in sales;
- it is also an offence to indicate, by whatever means, that the price is, in fact, less than the actual price; this takes in advertisements which do not include VAT in the price without indicating that VAT is payable.

Similar provisions apply to:

- the provision of any services, accommodation or facilities;

- the nature of the services;
- the timing and the location;
- the manner in which the services are provided.

Penalties under the Acts range from fines to imprisonment. In certain circumstances, a director, manager or secretary of a company can be held personally responsible.

The Acts set out two defences against prosecution. They both require that reasonable care should have been taken to check the accuracy of a statement. In the case of a company, an honest mistake by an employee in an organisation able to show that it takes reasonable precautions against such mistakes could be accepted as adequate defence. Similarly, a retailer able to show that he took reasonable measures to check the accuracy of statements made by a manufacturer would have a defence. A publication carrying a misleading advertisement would not normally be liable under the Act provided it could show that it had no reason to suspect it would amount to an offence.

The Trade Description Acts are enforced by local authorities under the direction of the Director-General of Fair Trading.

Fair Trading Act

The Act gives wide powers to the Director-General of Fair Trading for the protection of private consumers against unfair trading practices by anyone supplying goods and services.

If the Director-General considers that an unfair trading practice may exist he is empowered to call for an investigation. The result of the investigation has to be sent to the Department of Trade and Industry. The Minister is required to place the report before Parliament which may then approve a draft order giving effect to proposals contained in the report.

Consumer Credit Act

With some exceptions, the Act regulates consumer credit agreements of all kinds and lays down the formalities required for making them. The exceptions include consumer credit agreements secured on land; land mortgage agreements entered into with an insurance company, a friendly society, a trade union, an employers' association or a charity; agreements where the credit is repaid in four instalments or less; credit used in connection with overseas trade.

The Act requires that the person receiving the credit (including hire purchase agreements, cash loans and other financial accommodations):

- knows precisely the nature and the cost of the proposed agreement, including the cost of the credit;
- has a written agreement giving a clear account of his rights and obligations.

The agreement must:

- give the names of the parties to the agreement together with their addresses;
- state the amounts of all payments due and when and to whom they are payable;
- state the total charge for the credit;
- give the true annual rate of the total charge for the credit expressed as a percentage per annum;
- define the rights of the person receiving the credit to pay off the debt earlier than agreed.

Every copy of the agreement must contain all the terms and must give details of the debtor's rights, if any, to cancel the agreement. The debtor must sign the agreement in person and the agreement, as signed, must be completed in full before signature. The debtor must be given a copy of the agreement when he has signed it. If it is sent for signature and return a copy must accompany it at the same time.

(a) Hire purchase agreements

The Act imposes some restrictions on a finance company wishing to repossess goods when the debtor fails to make payment of instalments by due date.

- The finance company must supply the debtor with a default notice giving seven days in which to make the payments due.
- When more than one third of the agreed price has been paid by the debtor the finance company needs a court order to obtain repossession — unless the debtor has terminated the agreement.
- The finance company needs a court order before it can enter the debtor's house to take repossession.

(b) Marketing credit

The Act prescribes five situations in which criminal offences may be committed by a person carrying on a consumer credit business, while seeking to attract customers:

(1) It is an offence for any person carrying on a consumer credit business to canvass, by oral representation, cash loans, unless the negotiations take place on the trade premises of either party or unless the debtor has requested in writing a visit by the creditor.
(2) It is unlawful to send, but not give, to a minor any document inviting him to borrow money or obtain goods on credit; the sender has a defence if he can show that he did not know that the recipient was a minor.
(3) It is unlawful to send credit cards to persons who have not previously requested them unless the token cannot be used to provide credit exceeding £30 or unless the token is simply to replace a token previously sent or given unlawfully, under an existing credit agreement.
(4) For advertising, the Consumer Credit Act creates three offences:

(a) providing material information which is false or misleading;

(b) where the advertisement relates to the provision of goods or services, failure to state the cash price as well as the credit price; and

(c) infringing any of the requirements of the regulations made under the CCA controlling the content of advertisements. Broadly, the regulations divide advertisements into three classes (full, intermediate and simple) distinguished by the amount of information disclosed, and requires each class to conform to minimum requirements. Most importantly, if a creditor chooses to advertise his interest rates, they must be expressed in terms of an annual percentage rate.

(5) The provisions of the Act and the accompanying Regulations relating to the provision of quotations to prospective debtors correspond closely to the requirements for full credit advertisements; the creditor must disclose the cash price of the goods or services to be provided, the charge for credit expressed as an annual percentage rate and information as to any necessary securities, as well as a variety of other matters. It is an offence to give false or misleading information or to omit any information demanded by the law.

Direct mail

Marketing by direct mail, measured in terms of annual expenditure, ranks third, after press and television, in a breakdown of all advertising expenditure in the UK. Measured in terms of growth it ranks number one.

It is still a relatively new way of selling goods and services but a body of lore has built up on direct mail marketing and there are some generally accepted standards against which individual companies can measure their particular experience. One such standard suggests that the average direct mail campaign, reasonably well targeted and prepared ought to produce a response, in the form of either orders or of enquiries, of two per cent of the total number mailed. If it does not, it is said, the campaign was not directed at the right audience; or the sales letter and leaflet which make up most direct mail shots were wrongly written or presented; or the product being marketed was not attractive.

If this standard of response is accepted, a marketing department contemplating a direct mail campaign can make some advance projections. If, for example, it divides the total cost (postage, stationery, printing) per 1,000 mailings by the price of the product being marketed it has a line on the response it needs to break even on the exercise. If the answer is less than 20 — two per cent of the 1,000 mailed — direct mail may not be the best way of marketing the particular product.

These calculations suggest that, as a generalisation, direct mail may be best suited to higher priced products and services. On current costs, a product selling at much under £15 would need more than a two per cent response to produce a satisfactory result. The fact that response to a direct mail shot can, in most cases, be measured precisely, makes it an attractive marketing approach for many goods and services. But it is not necessarily a substitute for advertising through the press or television. It is not uncommon for a company to back up a press advertising campaign with a selective direct mail approach.

Another item in direct mail lore is that a mail shot received by a manager in his company office on Monday is very likely to remain un-read. Monday, it is said, is the heaviest post day of the week for most companies. It follows from this, that Monday may be the best day on which to post a mail shot, assuming next-day delivery by first-class mail. However, it is also said that the best months for mailings are January, February, March, September, October and November. This in turn indicates that since there are only 26 Mondays in these six months, a lot of competing sales literature arrives on managers' desks on the same 26 Tuesdays, always assuming next-day delivery.

It is widely accepted that the most effective direct mail shots comprise a sales letter addressed to the recipient by name plus an attractive sales leaflet or brochure. The sales letter, it is said, should tell the recipient why he should buy the product; the leaflet should explain what the product does and point out its qualities. It is also widely said that the length of the sales letter is immaterial to the success of the direct mail shot. A subsidiary view is that the length and general style of the sales letter must be dictated by the nature of the audience to which it is directed, and by the nature of the product or service being marketed. In this view, for example, a target audience of professionally qualified people would react best to a short sales letter and a more detailed description of the product being marketed. A target audience lower down the income scale might react best to a longer letter which extols more exuberantly the virtues of the product and a more flamboyant sales brochure. This approach follows an old marketing adage: sell the sizzle, not the sausage.

A summary of some of the accumulated wisdom built up around direct mail marketing includes the following points:

- address the recipient by name whenever possible;
- whatever the length of the sales letter, tell the recipient in the first paragraph why you think he should buy your product;
- a sales leaflet that includes an order form should include:
  (a) the marketing company's registration number;
  (b) the VAT payable, shown separately;
  (c) space for the signature of the person placing the order;
  (d) space for the amount of money that may, in cash with order forms, accompany the order to be written in;
  (e) a telephone contact in case of a query.
- include a reply-paid envelope in the mail shot: or supply a freepost address for the reply;
- follow up leads promptly.

Forecasting

Every business has to make forecasts. The range of forecasting techniques now available increases the chances of getting the forecast right: but no technique can do more than that. The accuracy of a forecast has to depend on the accuracy of the data used in making it, and on the amount of relevant data available.

One of the several very simple techniques is PERT, acronym for programme evaluation and review technique. It depends on estimates by an expert (who might be the sales manager) of optimistic (O), pessimistic (P) and most likely (ML) developments — sales revenue, for example. The three estimates are weighted, using a simple formula:

$$\text{Sales revenue} = \frac{O + P + 4ML}{6}$$

Although the technique is simple in its application and concept the fact that it is based on expert opinion is an important ingredient. The expert making the forecast is drawing on his experience and knowledge of the market. Apart from its simplicity PERT has the merit that it takes into account the reluctance even of experts to commit themselves to a single figure.

Expert opinion is used in a second technique known as the Delphi method. A panel of experts (sales managers, production managers, marketing managers) is each asked separately to respond in writing to a specific question such as an estimate of sales revenue for a new product. The experts are kept physically apart. Each member is then told the middle value of all the responses and, where appropriate, asked to explain why his estimate varies significantly from that middle value.

The panel members are then asked to submit answers to the questionnaire again and the process is repeated until all the estimates are within an acceptably narrow bracket. Because the method depends on keeping each expert unaware of what the other experts are forecasting it avoids some aspects of group behaviour in which one dominant member can influence the others.

Both these methods, depending as they do on subjective opinions, can be used to check other methods using statistics. For them, a basic technique, known as time series analysis, depends on accumulating data (sales revenue as often as not) for regular periods (monthly, weekly) over several years. These figures can then be plotted on a graph and will normally produce a zigzag graph line. Drawing a straight line through the middle of the zigzags will produce a trend line which can then be extended to cover the period being forecast. Such a projection assumes that the market will behave in the future as it has in the past. Since it rarely does behave in this way, some refinements are necessary. One is to draw a graph for the most recent data, draw a trend line and compare its slope with that of the trend line for the longer time scale graph. If there is a significant variation in the angles of the slope further refinements are needed. One is to identify the peaks and troughs of the zigzag graph line with the factors, external or internal, causing them. The factors can range from sickness in the sales force to mergers among a company's main customers. Since much sales forecasting is short term, the more accurately the reasons for peaks and troughs can be established, the more accurate the forecast.

It is widely believed that well formed patterns of market behaviour keep their shape for at least six months. Changes in general economic conditions do not normally produce short-term market changes. Nevertheless, developments such as changes in hire purchase terms, movements in excise duties or in the level of interest rates affect sales in a range of consumer goods.

It is not uncommon for a search for the factors causing peaks and troughs in sales revenue to throw up firm links between overall sales and the performance of a particular sector of a market. One case quoted is that of a large publishing company which established such a link between its overall advertising revenue with the rate of sale of second-hand cars and the number of job vacancies advertised. The inclusion of some of the variables affecting sales performance in forecasting based on past performance usually involves the use of a computer to create an econometric model. This opens up the possibilities of constantly adjusting the variables and of enabling management to ask 'what would happen if' questions.

Public relations

An American definition of public relations is that it means 'doing good and getting credit for it'.

It reflects acceptance of the fact that whether it is aware of it or not, every company has a public image. It forms, unbidden and unavoidably, from the way a company conducts its business: the quality of its products or services; the way the switchboard deals with incoming calls; delivery times; cleanliness of delivery vans; packaging; advertising style.

It follows from this that a prime concern of a public relations exercise is to identify any shortcomings which may be denting a company's public image and rectify them. This requires an appreciation of how the public sees the company or, more broadly, a particular sector of business. It is said, for example, that industry in general was slow to appreciate the growing weight of public concern over pollution. Further, that the response to that concern was defensive, despite the very considerable efforts by many companies to protect the environment.

In America, where the use of public relations consultants is more widespread than in Britain, many companies accept that public relations is a specific management function as important as any other area of management. It is common for United States companies of all sizes to have at least one person who is responsible, either full or part time, for the company's internal and external relationships.

Specific problems normally require specific solutions. A company about to declare a number of workers redundant, for example, has several problems: it has to explain, honestly and forthrightly, to its workforce why the redundancies are necessary; it has to ensure that the local (or national) press knows the reasons and does not draw the conclusion that the company is in serious trouble. It also has to take into account the local, social consequences of the redundancies, and to do what it can to soften the impact on the local community.

For a company with no specific problems to deal with, there are several options available for maintaining or enhancing a good public image.

Charities

Companies in general contribute only a very small proportion of all charitable giving in Britain. Most of it comes from individuals. The size of total donations to charity every year is such that it follows that many millions of people in Britain attach importance to charitable activities. It is open to companies to react to this situation by developing their own policy for charitable giving; and, having developed it, to make it known. For a local company, a declared adoption of a local charity may be the right option. For a national company, with a larger revenue, a more comprehensive policy is likely to be more appropriate. In some cases, donations to charities can attract tax benefits but the view is that this consideration should not weigh too heavily on companies contemplating a programme of donations.

Sponsorship

The big national and international companies are usually thought of as being natural sponsors of competitors in national events, or of the events themselves. For such companies with adequate budgets available, the fact that many regularly sponsor events of various kinds suggests they find sponsorship an effective part of their public relations activities.

But sponsorship is not necessarily confined to the big companies. A small company might well find it useful to improve industrial relations by sponsoring an employee entering the London Marathon, or some smaller local event. A professional firm, unable to advertise, can sponsor a seminar on a subject of concern to its main clients, actual or potential.

The media

The rule seems to be that if a company wants to get on television or in the press it should buy space and advertise. Public relations exercises designed to attract editorial comment are, in general, not very successful.

Nevertheless, despite the mass of press releases from a variety of organisations that land on a journalist's desk, each one is likely to be looked at — just in case. A company with something specific to communicate can, through a soberly written press release, attract a journalist's attention. Journalists are taught always to telephone for further details on any press release in which they are interested: a press release thus needs to include the name of the company's contact and a telephone number.

Pricing products and services

The behaviour of consumers in a particular market, taken as a whole, is always rational. A decision on prices for goods and services requires as complete an understanding as possible of all the factors resulting in that behaviour.

Many, perhaps most, companies use the cost-plus approach to arrive at an end-user price which will yield an acceptable return on the resources employed to produce goods and services. Many work backwards from the prices of competitive products and services to arrive at the cost level needed to undercut competitors on price.

If price were the only determinant of demand the conventional profit-maximising economic theory that price should be set at the point where marginal cost equals marginal revenue could be all that is needed. There would then be fewer company failures. But, because price is not the sole determinant of success, price decisions have to take in a variety of considerations:

- the pattern of consumer demand: small convenience items must be readily available and low-cost; small price differentials between competing products on a supermarket shelf can be critical;
- product life: prices of products with a finite shelf life require adjustment as time passes;
- demand elasticity: demand for essential commodities is only mildly affected by price rises although if the rises are too steep a search for substitutes can begin; consumption of non-essentials can react sharply to price movements;
- brand image: if a successful advertising and promotional campaign by a manufacturer can persuade consumers that a particular product has special advantages, the consumers may well buy it at a price well above those of competing products;
- distribution channels: the margins paid to the intermediaries in the marketing channels can be critical in achieving marketing objectives;
- availability of substitutes.

Current thinking is that all companies need to develop a cohesive pricing policy for their range of products or services as part of their overall business strategy.

Pricing

If a product or service fulfills the needs and expectations of the customer, he may jib at the price, but he will pay it — and come again. If he is offered an identical product or service at different prices, he will usually choose the higher-priced one.

It follows from these two basic principles that the best pricing policy is to sell at what the market will bear. Arriving at the correct level, however, can be a painful experience and methodology has been developed to minimise the possibilities of getting things badly wrong. Central to the methodology is the concept of price elasticity which measures the relationship of demand to price. Elasticity is said to equal unity when a percentage change in price results in the same percentage change in demand — in the opposite direction. A feel for the degree of elasticity in a particular market is, therefore, an essential first requirement in determining a pricing policy. There is no point in promoting special offers in a market which does not respond to price changes — an inelastic market.

Costing

Whatever its pricing policy, a company must know the cost of producing the product or service it is selling and a number of methods are used.

Absorption costing takes in all the costs plus a contribution to overheads plus an agreed profit margin; *direct costing* is much the same except that it includes all other costs such as promotion. Both methods are both useful and essential: they produce a price level below which the company cannot sell without incurring losses.

The other methods are a little more sophisticated. *Incremental costing* takes account of the costs involved in moving from one level of output to another, if rising demand means using more machinery, for example. *Marginal costing* is first cousin to incremental costing in that it takes in the actual production costs plus the selling cost of one extra unit or batch of products.

Opportunity costing makes allowance for a situation in which the same plant can be used to make two different products so that making one would mean foregoing the profit that might have been earned from the other.

Break-even analysis calculates the revenue required to cover all costs involved in production. *Mark-up pricing* is the traditional method of adding a mark-up agreed by custom and practice to a particular range of products. *Target pricing* sets a price that gives a required rate of return.

Each method has its adherents — and its pitfalls. A manufacturer who adds an acceptable profit margin to his total production costs will not know how much revenue he has lost because his selling price was not as high as his market would bear.

The market

Quality and price are important considerations in any market place but they are not the only factors. Underlying every buying decision is the buyer's perception of the risk involved in making a particular purchase.

A child with limited pocket money to spend will take a long time in deciding which sweets to buy. If he gets it wrong, he will have to wait a week — a long time in childhood — before he can correct it.

A wife buying a washing machine for the first time may have a limited budget but, within that budget, she will buy the machine that promises to offer the smallest risk of its going wrong. This may be the highest priced machine within her budget, and often is; it almost certainly will be the machine that offers the best guarantees against failure or the cheapest maintenance service.

The risk factor is accepted as being the single most important factor in buying decisions and full consideration of this element in each particular marketplace is vital in all pricing policies.

Product management

It appears to be widely accepted that most new products fail commercially. Nevertheless, virtually all companies go in for a new product sooner or later and there is nothing to suggest that the position will change much in the near future. What may be changing, however, is the way companies now set about acquiring ideas for new products and the way they subsequently screen those ideas. An underlying factor in new product management and development is that the people involved like something new. Anyone coming up with a new idea is likely to get a sympathetic first hearing.

For most companies, ideas for new products come mostly from either a technical specialist who has found a better way of doing something; or from the marketing department, whose sales force constantly pick up suggestions from their customers. For small companies, a flow of ideas from these sources may be enough. For larger companies able to finance an organised research and development programme, a more orderly approach to developing new ideas is possible.

It is open to all companies to use the brainstorming technique: a meeting of executives charged with producing any ideas, however fanciful, for the meeting to explore. The success of brainstorming is regarded as being dependent on the personalities of the executives involved. Somebody who produces too many fanciful ideas might arouse doubts over his competence.

However the ideas arise, it is widely held that new product development should be in the hands of one executive, backed by an adequate budget and with authority to require various departments to produce information and guidance. The argument is that an executive whose advancement in his company depends on getting things right, more often than not will be much more effective than a committee, where responsibility for success or failure is shared. An executive responsible for new products might well seek the advice of a committee but the decision on whether or not to recommend acceptance or rejection of a proposal to the board has to rest with him.

A product development manager, contemplating a new proposal, has to ask a number of questions:

- If the new product is successful, how might sales of the company's other products be affected?
- Does the competition have anything similar to the product proposed already on the market?
- Does the company have the resources in-house to handle the new product? What are the marketing department's views on taking on another product? What does the production department think would be involved?
- What are the likely sales of the new product?
- At the level of sales projected, what would be the unit cost of production? Marketing, administration and overheads costs?
- How does the price to the end-user indicated by these costing exercises compare with prices charged by the competition for any other product in broadly the same area?
- What do the company's main customers think of the idea?

Not many new products are really very new. A large proportion are adaptations or developments of existing products in a market where the main characteristics are known. Existing market data can be helpful in constructing forecast sales figures. With a totally new product — the ball-point pen, the jet engine, transistor radios — the customary forecasting techniques do not always apply. It is in these situations, when a company is venturing into uncharted territory, that an executive responsible for new product development has to make his stand.

Research

Current thinking on market research draws these conclusions:

- a surplus of marketing data, rather than too little, is a major problem for most managements;
- a distinction has to be drawn between market research (into markets for a specific product or service) and marketing research (systematic gathering of information about problems relating to the marketing of goods and services);
- marketing research for established products in a mature market is essential for maintaining and improving market share;
- market research for a new product helps to minimise the risk of launching it but provides an aid, not a substitute, for management decision;

- to avoid being flooded with useless data, managements must have a clear understanding of the information they need to help with a specific situation.

Cost

Market research for a new product, properly conducted, turns uncertainty into a risk which research results will help to put a figure on. If, for example, research results indicated that a new product had a 90 per cent chance of achieving a 20 per cent market share in two years from launch, management would have a basis on which to take a decision. If the development costs for that new product were £1 million, it could be worthwhile to spend up to £100,000 on further research that might help to reduce the risk of losing the investment. Decisions on the size of a research budget must be related to value placed on reducing the cost of failure.

Marketing research for an established product in a mature market is not concerned with risk assessment but in detecting market trends, shifts in consumer spending patterns, changes in market shares, performance of competing products. It is a continuous process which keeps management regularly in touch with the marketplace. Budgets for such research relate to product turnover in the market and it is sometimes helpful, in deciding on budget allocations, to consider what the loss in revenue would be following a one per cent fall in market share, remembering that research costs are tax deductible.

Desk research

It has become an axiom that all good research begins at home. A mass of data is either free or available at low cost from: government ministries, the HMSO, trade associations, specialist presses, information offices at chambers of commerce, commercial libraries; specialist bodies such as the professional institutes, educational authorities, foreign embassies; the OECD, the EC; United Nations and published market surveys.

However, recent research into the way companies mobilise the data available to them is taken as indicating that, despite the use of computers — or perhaps because of it — this is one of the most badly organised areas of management. This, it is said, is because managements tend to fail to define precisely just what their information needs are. A consequence is that much more information is collected than is really needed.

Four requirements are suggested as a guide to constructing a cost-effective internal marketing information system:

- construction of a detailed list of all current data produced, or available;

50

- a listing, by each manager concerned, of the decisions he has to make plus the information needed to help make those decisions;
- consolidation of these needs to exclude duplications and redundant data;
- evaluation of the costs of providing the resulting information flow, thinking total but planning piecemeal to take into account future market developments that may demand modifications.

External research

It is widely accepted that external research, done mostly by sampling a small proportion of a market universe, is best done by a specialist outside company.
  Sampling usually takes one of three possible forms:

- face-to-face interviews between a trained interviewer and a selected list of respondents within the target profile; the method is regarded as producing the most worthwhile results but it is time-consuming and costly;
- postal questionnaires enable a larger proportion of the market universe to be covered but responses can vary from a few per cent up to 30 per cent or so, with 40 per cent commonly regarded as exceptionally good;
- telephone interviews are seen as being best suited to very short enquiries that need factual responses, not opinions or views.

Bias

Because market research as a management discipline is still developing, current thought is that its findings have to be treated with discretion. There are some pitfalls: an enthusiastic originator of a new product idea may have a bias towards interpreting the results of market research as favouring go-ahead, for example. A less obvious example is the difficulty of asking a sample audience the right questions in a way that will mean the same thing to all of them.

Restrictive trade practices

Any agreement between two parties concerning:

- (a) prices charged for; and
- (b) terms and conditions for supplying goods and services must be registered with the Director General of Fair Trading.

Such agreements are entered on a public register and may, in certain cases, be referred to the Restrictive Practices Court. The parties concerned must then satisfy the court that their agreement is not contrary to the public interest. If they fail to do so they must stop giving effect to the restrictions.

Goods

The relevant legislation (Restrictive Trade Practices Act 1976) covers:

- prices, charges;
- terms or conditions on which people are to do business;
- the quantities or descriptions of goods to be produced, supplied or acquired;
- the manufacturing process to be used, or the levels or the amounts of goods to be manufactured;
- the persons with whom business is to be done;
- the areas or places of the business.

Services

Similar provisions apply to services, but with some exemptions. These include exclusive dealing agreements, trade mark agreements, patents and registered designs, know-how agreements, copyright agreements. In general, restrictions in the professional services are not registrable where they concern, for example, the fixing of charges for accounting and auditing services.

Sale, contract of

No particular formality is required in law for a contract of sale: the parties can insert whatever terms they please. There are, however, certain terms which the law implies. These are:

(a) The seller has the right to sell the goods.
(b) The goods are free of any encumbrance or charge not known to the buyer.
(c) The goods comply with the description; even when the buyer selects the goods, the sale may still be a sale by description.
(d) In a sale in course of business:
    (i) the goods shall be of merchantable quality, i.e. as fit for the purpose or purposes for which goods of that kind are commonly bought as it is reasonable to expect having regard to any description applied to them, the price (if relevant) and all the other relevant circumstances;
    (ii) the goods shall be fit for the purpose for which the seller knows they are intended. This condition is not implied when it was not reasonable for the buyer to have relied on the skill or judgment of the seller.
(e) When the sale is by sample, the bulk shall correspond with the sample.

Some of the main points of contract law are listed below.

- When goods are in the possession of a third party (e.g. a warehouse keeper) at the time of the sale, delivery is deemed to take place when the third party acknowledges that he is now holding the goods on behalf of the buyer.
- When a contract requires or authorises the seller to deliver goods to the buyer, delivery to a carrier is equivalent to delivery to the buyer.
  - (a) The seller must make a proper contract with the carrier.
  - (b) When goods are to be transported by sea, the seller must give notice to the buyer to enable him to insure the goods. In the absence of notice, the risk of loss or damage is on the seller.
- The risk of loss or damage to the goods is usually on the party who has title to the goods at the time of the loss or damage. The contract of sale may stipulate when the risk of loss or damage is to pass.
- If the goods have been received by the buyer who does not pay, all the seller can do is to sue for the price unless the contract of sale contains a stipulation that title is not to pass until payment.
- If the seller transfers the goods to a carrier and then becomes aware that the buyer is insolvent, there is a right of stoppage in transit that will allow the seller to resume possession of the goods until payment. An insolvent buyer is one who has ceased to pay his debts or cannot pay debts as they become due.
- When goods are sold on approval or on sale or return, title passes when the buyer indicates approval or acceptance. Any act inconsistent with the seller's continued ownership is deemed to be acceptance. Acceptance is also shown by retention of the goods beyond the stipulated period or for an unreasonable time.

Sales management

Sales management is perhaps the most difficult, probably the most critical and certainly the most dynamic of all management functions. Nevertheless, like most management functions, effective sales management is based on four main fundamentals: planning, co-ordinating, controlling and motivating.

Planning

Construction of a written and comprehensive sales plan, regarded as an essential first step for all sales management operations, requires:

- identification of the company's heavy-use, light and periodic customers;
- research to ensure that the company's products or services are those that

the heavy-use customers want, in the form provided and at the cost available;

- critical comparison of the company's products with those of the competition;
- identification of changes, current or potential, in the market;
- identification of environmental influences on the market that are outside the company's control;
- determination of the size of the market, the company's share in it, competitor's shares, trends.

Underlying all sales planning lies the basic sales and marketing concept that the customer is central in the sales management function. This concept was presented schematically in a book by E J McCarthy, *Basic marketing: a managerial approach*, published in 1978.

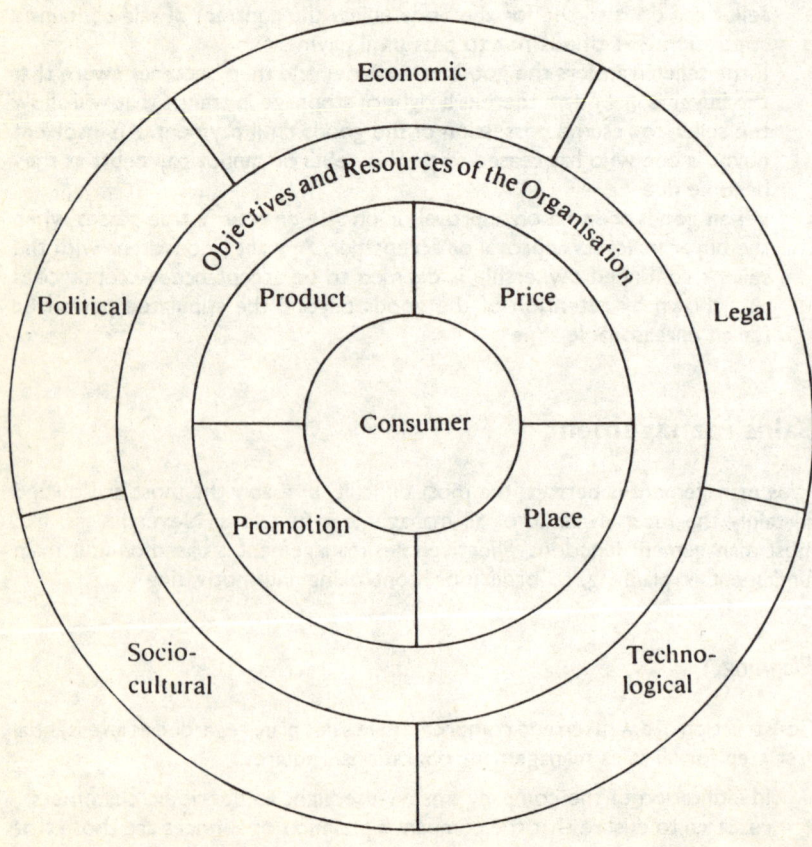

The outer ring in the diagram covers those areas over which a sales manager has very little, if any, control. They are, nevertheless, factors which must be taken into account in drawing up a sales plan. They are normally identified as:

- *Economic:* includes the distribution of per capita GNP; regional unemployment; inflation; changes in taxation; regional business environment.
- *Political:* the respective roles of the private and public sectors in both the country as a whole and in particular regions can be a decisive influence in formulating sales plans. To the extent that changes in national government normally herald changes in economic policy, different regions can react differently to such changes.
- *Socio-cultural:* with real incomes rising faster than inflation for those in jobs, the general level of disposable income has been rising for some years. The impact on consumer demand has varied from region to region and in response to the development of new technologies, such as the arrival of relatively low cost home computers.
- *Technological:* keeping pace with the latest innovations is normally not enough to ensure a company's survival; the need is for a company to recognise its particular competence within a particular field and respond accordingly.
- *Legal:* any company has to be aware of the legal constraints, general and specific, within which it must operate; the requirements imposed as a result of membership of the EEC are becoming steadily more obtrusive and failure to conform with them can attract severe penalties.

It is within these constraints that any company, irrespective of size, must establish, first, its corporate objectives and, then, the sales objectives which must be achieved to achieve those objectives.

It is commonly accepted that the key to an effective market strategy lies in identifying the heavy-user sectors of a company's markets and directing the company's products towards those sectors. A number of variables are available for describing market segments: for consumer markets they are often listed as follows:

- *Geographic:*   standard planning regions
  TV regions
  urban/rural
- *Demographic:*   age
  sex
  income
  occupation
  education
  socio-economic group
- *Personal:*   life style
  personality

Essential Facts for Managers

- *Behaviour:* user status
      usage rate
      purchase occasions
      readiness stage

More recently, there have been rapid developments in techniques for segmenting markets. One carries the acronym ACORN (A Classification of Residential Neighbourhoods). This involves an analysis on a mix of variables from the national census to create neighbourhood types.

However a market may be segmented, each identified segment requires separate consideration.

Size: if the size of a market segment cannot be established (and, thereby, its potential) it may be best to ignore it.

Access: if a segment cannot be reached through some established promotional channel, the cost of special promotion may be unacceptable.

The available mix of means whereby a company promotes its products is usually made up of four factors: advertising; personal selling; sales promotions of various kinds; publicity. What proportion of a company budget is devoted to any of these items will be related to its products and its markets. It is, however, widely accepted that the total budget must be sufficiently large to achieve the objectives set. Budgets based on percentages of sales or on meeting the activities of competitors are rarely satisfactory.

Co-ordination

There are three basic ways of co-ordinating the efforts of a sales force (*see* diagrams):

- Line organisation: the sales manager communicates directly with each member of his sales force either personally or through an assistant.
- Line-staff organisation: authority flows direct from the sales manager to each member of the sales force but staff assistants exist to offer advice and support to the sales force without any authority to issue instructions.
- Functional organisation: similar to a line-staff organisation except that more than one of the subordinate line managers may issue instructions to the sales force.

Sales territories

It is commonly accepted that a selection of sales territories should be based on regions or areas for which regional or area statistics are readily available. Although these statistics may be no more than indicative they may provide a basis from which a company can draw some tentative conclusions on its perfor-

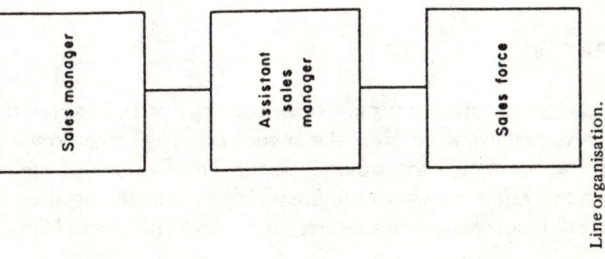

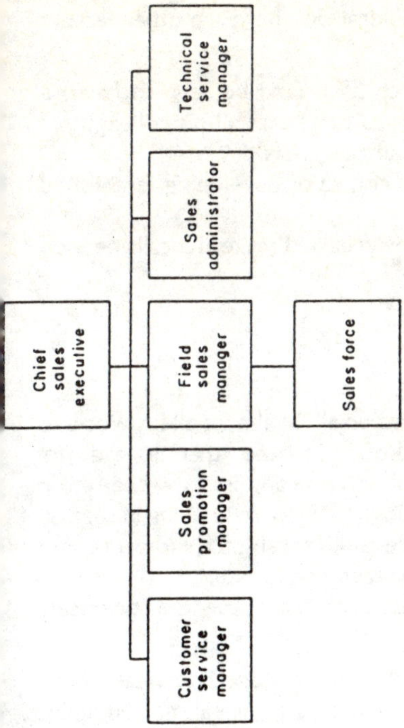

Line and staff organisation.

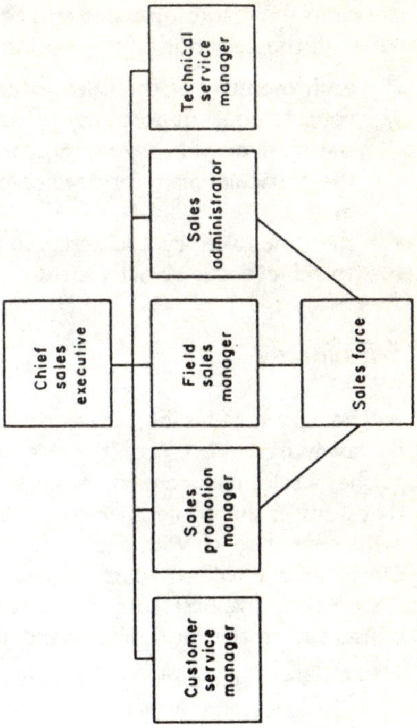

Functional organisation.

Line organisation.

mance in the market. Beyond this basic consideration, there are other factors to guide the selection of territories:

- each member of the sales force needs to have (and be seen to have) a roughly equal opportunity of reaching sales targets as all his colleagues;
- the number of heavy-use customers in various areas;
- the particular plans for developing new accounts or developing established ones;
- the time taken by a salesman to travel the area and make the calls needed to achieve the objectives set.

Sales force

By the nature of his job, a salesman spends either all or almost all his working day away from his office. It is this single and obvious factor that alone distinguishes a salesman from any other member of his company. It is also the factor that dictates that a sales manager must give a high priority to keeping in regular and frequent touch with each of his sales force and, thereby, to help overcome the various problems which a lone-wolf existence can create.

The extensive literature written about these problems presents a convincing consensus on the more important ones:

- A salesman needs to be given the authority to negotiate deals, offer discounts and, in general, be able to appear as a principal, not an agent needing to check with higher authority, in his dealings with customers.
- However much he may enjoy freedom from immediate supervision, a salesman shares with others the need to feel he belongs. Sales managers satisfy this need by keeping the sales force informed on developments, personal visits, letters, phone calls and regular circulars.
- Most salesmen react well to being set realistic targets: it helps to remove uncertainty.
- Salesmen are motivated by their belief that reward should be equated with effort. Nevertheless, their need to feel secure in their jobs is no less than that of others in different areas of corporate life. Achieving agreed targets makes for a feeling of security.

Trade marks

The law imposes no duty on manufacturers or traders to register their trade marks. However, registration gives the owner of a registered trade mark the right to ask the courts to stop others using it. The owner of an unregistered trade mark may be left only with the possibility of proceeding at common law for 'passing off' if somebody else misuses his mark. The Trade Marks Registry, a branch of the Patent Office, requires that, before a mark can be registered, it must be distinctive of the goods to which it applies.

The Registry classifies goods into 34 classes and, if registration of a mark is required for more than one of these classes, more than one application is needed.

Once the Registry is satisfied on the distinctiveness of the mark for which application is made, it searches the register for any similar marks. If the search reveals nothing the mark is then advertised in *The Trade Marks Journal*. If no-one opposes the application and the registration fee is paid the trade mark is registered. The registration remains in force for seven years and may be subsequently renewed for successive periods each time of 14 years. The process of registration normally takes at least eight months.

Passing off

An action for passing off would be based not on statute but on common law. In general terms, it is actionable for anybody to try to pass off goods as those of somebody else.

3 Personnel

Absence

The need for companies to monitor all absences is fundamental. Clear rules for employees to observe as part of their employment contract are essential to any monitoring system. Staff also need to know that a breach of the rules will be considered a disciplinary offence. Points to be included in these rules are as follows:

- how, to whom and how quickly to report sick;
- how to comply with the company's rules for self-certification;
- provision for employees to be referred to the company's medical adviser as necessary;
- how to apply for annual leave;
- how to apply for special leave, for example time off for public duties or for compassionate reasons.

Line managers and supervisors must be responsible for recording the absences of their subordinate staff and notifying whoever keeps the records. The latter must ensure that the supervisors are aware when employees who report to them reach unacceptable levels of absence.

Measuring absence

An ACAS booklet entitled *Absence* says that the most common measure of absence is the *lost time rate* which shows absence from all causes in a given period as a percentage of the total time available by using the following equation:

$$\frac{\text{Total absence (hours/days) in the period}}{\text{Possible hours (or days) available}} \times 100 = \text{Lost time rate (\%)}$$

On its own, the lost time rate can obscure the problem of a small number of people absent for long periods, or a larger number frequently absent for short periods. So, says ACAS, the frequency rate can be measured for a given period to show the average number of absences per employees in the group as follows: as follows:

$$\frac{\text{No. of spells of absence in the period}}{\text{No. of employees}} \times 100 = \text{Frequency rate (\%)}$$

An individual frequency rate showing the number of employees absent during a given period can also be assessed by using the following equation:

$$\frac{\text{No. of employees having one or more spells of absence}}{\text{Total number of employees}} \times 100 = \text{Individual frequency rate (\%)}$$

In addition to these broad measures absence records should be regularly analysed to identify, for example, departmental and seasonal variations or characteristics of the employees with the poorest absence records.

ACAS

The Advisory Conciliation and Arbitration Service was established as an independent statutory body by the Employment Protection Act 1975. It is governed by a Council which includes representatives of the TUC and CBI. The general duty of ACAS is to promote the improvement of industrial relations. Specific duties are to:

- encourage the extension, development and, where necessary, the reform of collective bargaining;
- provide conciliation in trade disputes;
- provide conciliation on all matters which could be the subject of proceedings before an industrial tribunal;
- arbitrate in disputes at the request of at least one party and with the agreement of the others;
- appoint mediators to offer assistance to the parties in a dispute;
- provide specific and general advice on industrial relations matters;
- issue codes of practice.

The objective of *conciliation* is to help the parties to reach a settlement which is mutually acceptable. *Arbitration* requires that both parties request the arbitrator to make an award which they undertake to accept. *Mediation* involves making recommendations and leaving the parties to make a settlement.

Conciliation officers also act in individual cases. They are required to try to settle complaints made by individuals that their rights under employment legislation have been infringed, without recourse to an industrial tribunal.

Once a claim has been made to a tribunal a conciliation officer will act if requested to do so by one of the parties or in any case where he thinks that there is a reasonable prospect of a settlement. He must first seek the reinstatement or re-engagement of the claimant unless he does not want to go back to the employer in which case the conciliation officer will try to get agreement on compensation.

If an agreement is reached both parties will be asked to sign an *ACAS COT 3* form and then the claimant may no longer bring his complaint to a tribunal, except in very exceptional circumstances.

The individual is able to ask a conciliation officer to assist while he is still in employment and before he has made a tribunal claim providing what he is complaining about could be the subject of such a claim.

In cases of collective dispute ACAS may provide for arbitration if all the parties agree and normally having first established that conciliation is unlikely to succeed and all internal disputes procedures have been exhausted. Arbitration awards are not legally binding although normally respected. Many company/ union procedures include reference to arbitration by ACAS as the final stage of their disputes procedure. ACAS maintains a list of individuals experienced in industrial relations who are willing to act as arbitrators and mediators. Their fees and expenses are borne by ACAS.

The Central Arbitration Committee (CAC)

Arbitration by ACAS can be carried out either by independent arbitrators or by the CAC whose members are nominated by ACAS to the Secretary of State for Employment including representatives of the unions and employers' interests. The CAC also has the statutory duty to hear complaints made by recognised independent trade unions that an employer has failed to disclose information necessary for the purposes of collective bargaining. The CAC also has the statutory power to amend collective agreements which are shown to discriminate against either men or women.

ACAS also operates a regional advisory service to help companies with industrial relations issues.

ACAS has powers to produce codes of practice which have been approved by Parliament. Industrial tribunals are required to take account of any provision in a code which is relevant to any question arising in the proceedings when determining that question.

Codes issued are:

* *Disciplinary practice and procedures in employment*
* *Disclosure of information to trade unions for collective bargaining purposes*
* *Time off for trade union activities and procedures*

ACAS has also published a series of advisory booklets:

* *Job evaluation*
* *Introduction to payment systems*
* *Personnel records*
* *Labour turnover*
* *Absence*
* *Recruitment and selection*
* *Induction of new employees*
* *Workplace communications*
* *The company handbook*
* *Employment policies*

Apprentices

A contract of apprenticeship must be in writing and is usually signed by the employer, the apprentice and the parent or guardian.

During the apprenticeship the employer is held to be acting *in loco parentis* and dismissal of an apprentice should take place only in exceptional circumstances such as gross misconduct involving a serious safety risk.

As an apprenticeship is legally a fixed-term contract it can include a waiver clause by which an apprentice signs away the right to claim unfair dismissal if no job is offered on completion of the apprenticeship.

If no job is available the apprentice is not redundant because he has never been employed in the capacity in which redundancy is claimed. However an apprentice dismissed during training because the employer no longer requires an apprentice could claim redundancy.

In the absence of a waiver clause an employer faced with a claim of unfair dismissal because he has not offered employment on the completion of training would have to show that he acted reasonably, for example, that there was no job that he could reasonably offer and that he gave the apprentice some warning that this was likely to be the case.

Arbitration

Recourse to arbitration is a voluntary alternative to litigation over a dispute between the parties to a contract. The arbitration award, provided it is within the law, is enforceable only when the parties have agreed that it should be so. Arbitration may or may not be less expensive than litigation, depending on the circumstances: but it is usually quicker as a means of resolving a dispute.

If the parties to a dispute agree beforehand to be bound by an arbitration decision given by a body or individual previously agreed upon by both parties, there is no appeal against that decision. Either party is free to appeal to a court on a point of law which may arise as a consequence of the award but the court has no power to set aside that award unless it is unlawful. In its strictest sense, arbitration, to be effective as a means of settling disputes, requires that both parties agree to be bound by the arbitrator's findings.

Where no such agreement exists, recourse to arbitration may help the parties along the path to arriving at their own resolution of the dispute between them. But the arbitrator's decision will not be binding.

The law distinguishes between a dispute and a failure to agree, but the distinction is occasionally blurred. The most commonly used test is whether the issue can be resolved by an expert or professional person (a chartered surveyor, for example, asked to give an opinion in a disputed rent review) or whether the dispute requires a judgment based on the evidence and arguments produced by the disputing parties.

Associated employer

A number of individual legal rights, for example to a redundancy payment, or to bring a complaint of unfair dismissal, require a certain length of continuous service with an employer, including any service with an associated employer.

Two employers are associated if one is directly or indirectly controlled by the other or if both are controlled by a third person, either directly or indirectly.

Attachment of earnings

A High Court, County Court or Magistrates' Court can serve an *Attachment of Earnings Order* on an employer requiring him to deduct a certain amount from an employee's weekly or monthly pay and send the amount to the collecting officer of the court. These orders are made to secure payment of maintenance, fines etc., and the employer is legally obliged to comply unless he has informed the court that he no longer employs the particular employee.

An order is in two parts: it specifies the amount to be deducted each week or month but it may also specify that the employee's take-home pay must not fall below a certain amount per week. If earnings vary from week to week the employer has to deduct a varying amount to maintain the take-home pay level and also to discharge the debt. The employer can deduct an extra 50p per day to cover administrative expenses.

Ballots

Ballots can be initiated and conducted by employers or by trade unions, or there can be joint co-operation on the preparation and conduct of them. Much depends on the questions being put and on the secrecy of the ballot.

Where there is a jointly organised secret ballot, the scope for the employer or the union later to claim that the results were suspect because the questions were loaded should be minimal.

Trade union ballots

Payments can be made to independent trade unions by the *Certification Officer* towards the unions' expenditure in connection with ballots which are so conducted as to secure, so far as is reasonably practicable, that those voting may do so in secret, provided that these are for:

- obtaining decisions or views from members about calling or ending a strike or other industrial action, including pre-industrial action ballots meeting the requirements of s.8 of the Trade Union Act 1984;
- union elections in accordance with union rules, including elections of voting members to principal executive committees meeting the requirements of s.2 of the Trade Union Act 1984;

67

- elections, as provided for in union rules, to the positions of president, chairman, secretary or treasurer or to any position which the person elected will hold as an employee of the union concerned;
- amending union rules;
- obtaining a decision about the amalgamation of a union with another union, or the transfer of a union to another union;
- obtaining decisions or views from members about accepting or rejecting an employer's offer in relation to their contractual terms and conditions of employment or other aspects of their relationship, including proposals about pay, hours of work, level of performance, holidays or pensions;
- such other purposes as the Secretary of State may specifically order.

Ballots to decide the extent of support for a union membership agreement do not qualify for payments.

To qualify for payments the arrangements for the conduct of the ballots must require that each voter marks his paper and returns it by post direct to the trade union conducting the ballot or to another person responsible for counting the votes.

Application for payments

If a union makes an application and the Certification Officer is satisfied that it relates to a ballot which meets the conditions, he also must satisfy himself on a number of points:

- The handling of the ballot did not contravene the union's rules, and any rules concerning the conduct of the ballot were complied with.
- If the ballot was to ascertain the extent of support for calling a strike or other industrial action, it was conducted in accordance with s.8 of the Trade Union Act 1984.
- If the ballot was to ascertain the extent of support for ending a strike or other industrial action, it was conducted to secure that all union members who were already participating in it were entitled to vote.
- Those entitled to vote were allowed to do so without inference or constraint.
- As far as reasonably practicable, those entitled to vote had a fair opportunity of doing so.
- Where the votes have been counted, they were fairly counted.
- If the ballot was for elections to the principal executive committee of a union, it was conducted in accordance with s.2 of the Trade Union Act 1984.

Expenditure covered

Payments towards the expenditure incurred by a union will be made by the Certification Officer in respect of:

(a) *Stationery and Printing* which includes voting papers, envelopes for sending them out and returning them, any other envelopes used to secure the secrecy of the voting, material enclosed with the voting papers which explains the matter to be voted upon or which relates to the procedure for voting. If the Certification Officer considers that the expenditure on these materials was unreasonable, he can restrict his payment to the amount he considers reasonable.

(b) *Postal costs* which are:
  (i) the amounts spent on second class post, or a cheaper means if this was used, or second class post if a more expensive means was used unless the Certification Officer considers that the more expensive means was reasonable in the circumstances when he may meet the amount spent; and
  (ii) similarly calculated payments for returning voting papers by post, subject to the condition that the payments will be limited to second class post if a prepaid letter post was used which cost more than that.

The Certification Officer can refuse to meet the additional postal costs if he considers that the weight of the material sent by post was unreasonable. He can look not only at the quantity of the material, but also at how the printing on it is spaced out and at the quality of the paper itself.

No secret ballot payments will be made by the Certification Officer until six weeks after whichever is the later of the following dates:

• the date when the results of the ballot were made known to the persons entitled to vote;
• the date an application for payment was made to the Certification Officer;
• the date on which an application to register an instrument of amalgamation or transfer has been made or, where there is an objection, the date of an order by the Certification Officer specifying the steps which must be taken before he will entertain an application to register the instrument.

Obligations on employers

When a union which is recognised by an employer for collective bargaining proposes to conduct any secret ballot which meets the requirements of the scheme described and the union asks the employer to allow his premises to be used for the voting by the employees who are members of the union, the employer must comply with the request as far as is reasonably practicable. If the number of persons employed by the employer — whether or not they are union members — does not exceed 20, including the number of employees of an associated employer, the employer may decline to allow his premises to be used for the ballot.

A union can complain to an industrial tribunal that, having asked an employer for the use of his premises so that a secret ballot can be held, the employer failed to comply with the request even though it was reasonably practicable for him to so do. If a joint employer/union ballot is conducted, the union's share of the cost would be reimbursable, but not the employer's share.

The Bridlington Agreement

When there is a dispute between two affiliated unions about the alleged poaching of the members of one by the other the TUC Disputes Committee acts as arbitrator following the principles laid down in the 1939 Bridlington Agreement and now revised into the *TUC Principles Governing Relations Between Unions.*

The main principles are set out below.

- Each union shall consider developing joint working agreements with unions with whom they are in frequent contact and in particular procedures for resolving specific issues and arrangements concerning spheres of influence, transfers of members and benefit rights, recognition of cards and demarcation of work. For example, unions should have regard to the interest of other unions which may be affected when negotiating sole recognition rights and closed shop agreements.
- No one who has recently been a member of any affiliated union should be accepted into membership of any other without enquiry of his present or former union. There are procedures to follow if the latter objects to a transfer of membership.
- No union shall organise activities at any establishment for a grade or grades of membership in which another union has the majority of workers employed and negotiates terms and conditions, except by agreement with that union.
- In the case of inter-union disputes no official strike should take place before the TUC has been able to examine the issue. If action short of a strike takes place the TUC must be informed immediately.
- If an inter-union dispute has led to an unauthorised stoppage of work there is an obligation on the union or unions concerned to resume normal working and to inform the TUC of their efforts to achieve this.

Business transfers

The Transfer of Undertakings (Protection of Employment) Regulations 1981 relate to the rights of employees when their employer's business or undertaking changes hands. An 'undertaking' is defined as any trade or business, or a part of one, which is a commercial concern.

Employees employed in the transferred undertaking immediately before the transfer are automatically transferred along with the business with all their contractual rights, except those under occupational pension schemes, and with their continuity of service preserved for both contractual and statutory purposes. This contrasts with sales of going concerns which are not relevant transfers. In this situation, unless the purchaser agrees to offer a job to the employees, the vendor is liable to pay a redundancy payment. If the new owner does take on the employees there is no right to a redundancy payment and the employee is treated as having continuity of service. If the assets only are sold and there is no going concern employees are entitled to redundancy payments from the vendor even if the new owner employs them immediately.

If an employee offered a job by a new owner refuses the offer his entitlement to a redundancy payment would depend on whether he had been offered suitable alternative employment which he unreasonably refused.

If employees are made redundant at the time of the transfer the liability to make a redundancy payment falls on the new owner.

An employee transferred with his contractual rights and obligations preserved has no claim that he can bring to an industrial tribunal but if the new employer substantially changes his terms and conditions he has the right to leave and claim constructive dismissal.

Collective agreements made between the company selling the undertaking and a union will still have the same effect after the transfer as if the purchasing company had made the agreement in the first place. Collective agreements incorporated into individual contracts will continue to apply until negotiated.

Recognition rights of unions automatically transfer to the new employer providing the undertaking transferred maintains a separate identity within the new employer's undertaking. However if the purchaser varies or rescinds the agreement there are no sanctions provided by the legislation although individual employees may be able to claim that this would be in breach of their contracts.

Dismissal

The Regulations provide that any employee, whether transferred to the new owner or an existing employee of the new owner, is deemed to be unfairly dismissed if 'the transfer or a reason connected with it is the reason or principal reason for his dismissal' unless there is 'an economic, technical or organisational reason entailing changes in the workforce of either the transferor or the transferee' when the employer may have to show an industrial tribunal that in these circumstances the dismissal was reasonable.

With no definition of what these terms mean in the legislation, tribunals have had considerable difficulty interpreting the Regulations and a body of case law is developing.

Consultation rights for unions

Where there is a recognition agreement with an independent trade union in respect of the employees who will be affected by a transfer the current employer must inform the union representatives of:

- the fact that the transfer is to take place, approximately when this will happen and the reasons for it;
- the legal, economic and social implications of the transfer for the affected employees;
- the measures which the employer envisages he will take in relation to the affected employees;
- the measures which the purchaser envisages he will take in relation to those employees which become his employees after the transfer.

There is an obligation on the purchaser to supply the vendor with the information he needs to meet this requirement.

The employer must then:

- consider any representations made by the union;
- reply to the representations and if he rejects any, state his reasons for this.

Certification Officer

The Certification Officer is appointed by the Secretary of State for Employment under the Employment Protection Act 1975. He is independent of both the Department of Employment and ACAS, the Advisory, Conciliation and Arbitration Service, although the latter provide support services.

His duties involve:

- maintaining lists of independent trade unions and employers' organisations;
- determining the independence of trade unions;
- seeing that unions and employers' organisations keep accounting records, have their accounts properly audited and submit annual returns;
- ensuring the periodic actuarial examination and separate funding of members' superannuation schemes;
- securing the observance of the statutory procedures for the mergers of unions and employers' organisations;
- administering the scheme by which public funds are provided for trade union secret ballots before industrial action and for elections to executive committees;
- examining complaints that a union has failed to comply with its legal duty to maintain a register of members, hold elections for members of its principal executive committee and conduct ballots for those elections as legally required.

Check off

Check off is the practice by which an employer collects union dues from employees direct from the pay of the employees and on behalf of the union. A union member may write to his employer stating that either he is exempt from the obligation to contribute to the union's political fund or that he has notified the union of his objection to contributing to it. On receipt of such notification the employer must ensure that he does not deduct the political levy. If the employer does not comply the employee can make a complaint to the county court (sheriff court in Scotland).

Children, employment of

For the purpose of legislation relating to the employment of children, a child is someone who is not over the compulsory school leaving age, currently 16. The legislation requires that:

- No child under the age of 13 may be employed in any capacity, regardless of whether he is paid or not.
  There are exceptions: a child under 12 may be employed by his parent or guardian in light agricultural or horticultural work; and local authorities can licence children to appear in an entertainment performance although no licence is required for school events.
- No child can be employed before 7.00 am or after 7.00 pm, or for more than two hours on a school day or a Sunday, or before the end of school hours on a school day.
- The total weekly working hours of children must not exceed 44.
- Children may not be employed in industrial undertakings (basically mining and quarrying, manufacturing and construction, transport including the transport of goods) unless only members of the same family are employed there.

Compensation

In many cases of alleged unfair or wrongful dismissal employer and employee come to an agreement about a termination package without recourse to the courts but such settlements usually follow the same principles as court awards.

Agreed termination packages are usually made under the aegis of a conciliation officer of the Advisory, Conciliation and Arbitration Service. The reason for this is that, legally, employees cannot sign away their rights to sue their employers through the employment courts, except where their agreement to refrain from presenting a case, or from proceeding with a complaint already made, is the result of action taken by the conciliation officer. Such settlements are usually made using a form of words in a separate, signed letter by which the employee also gives up the right to sue through the civil courts.

When an employee wins a claim for unfair dismissal before an industrial tribunal the award is normally in two parts: the basic award which is calculated in the same way as a statutory redundancy payment and the compensatory award which is 'such amount as the tribunal consider just and equitable in all the circumstances having regard to the loss sustained by the complainant in consequence of the dismissal in so far as that loss is attributable to action taken by the employer'.

The loss includes 'any expenses reasonably incurred by the complainant in consequence of the dismissal, and . . . the loss of any benefit which he might reasonably be expected to have had but for the dismissal'. It is important to note that:

- 'Just and equitable in *all* the circumstances' means that a tribunal can make a nil award if it considers this appropriate even if the employee has suffered loss. For example, where an employee was guilty of misconduct before dismissal, but the employer was unaware of this at the time, and based the reasons for dismissal on a different instance of misconduct.
- The compensatory award is subject to a maximum which is currently £8,000.
- The principle is to compensate the employee for loss, not to fine the employer.

The National Industrial Relations Court (NIRC) set out the main principles of assessing loss in the case of *Norton Tool Co Ltd* v *Tewson* in 1972.

This established the points that an employee is not entitled to compensation for injury to pride or feelings and that once found to have been unfairly dismissed, the burden of proving loss rests with the employee, not the employer.

Dismissal

It is a common misconception that *wrongful dismissal* is directly comparable with unfair dismissal except that the route is through the civil courts, not the employment courts. This is not so.

Most contracts of employment provide, explicitly or implicitly, for dismissal with due notice by the employer or resignation with due notice by the employee. There are exceptions, for example it has been held that certain university lecturers have guaranteed employment to normal retirement age. Under common law employees can therefore be dismissed if proper notice is given (or without notice in the case of gross misconduct which breaches the contract in that way). Wrongful dismissal is therefore primarily dismissal in breach of the notice terms and the employee can sue for damages which are calculated as loss incurred as a result of the employer's action during the notice period only.

The other circumstance where wrongful dismissal can be claimed is if the dismissal procedure has been breached, for example if all the stages have not been carried out. In this case damages will be limited to the loss during a period which would have enabled all these stages to have been completed, plus the notice period if no notice was given.

There are certain complications but in broad terms the calculations of compensation for unfair dismissal and damages for wrongful dismissal are on the same basis. Both relate to actual loss in terms of pay and benefits offset by other earnings and state benefits, as there is a requirement on claimants to take reasonable steps to reduce (or 'mitigate') their loss, for example by actively seeking other employment.

Pay

With loss of salary or wages the comparison is with what it might reasonably have been expected that the employee would have received net, during the period of loss. Loss includes an assessment of commission, overtime payments, shift premia, production bonuses, etc.

Immediate loss of earnings is taken at the date of the tribunal hearing and is therefore actual loss, net of other earnings, state benefits and any payment in lieu. The whole period is assessed, not week by week, so if the claimant is initially employed and then finds a job at a higher salary the sum total of new earnings is taken. If the employee loses a new job before the tribunal hearing, then further losses will not be taken into account if he or she lost this job through his or her own fault or for some other reason which is not the fault of the previous employer. However if, for example, the employee loses the second job because of redundancy on a last-in first-out basis, the tribunal may hold that this was due to the loss of the first job and take the second period of unemployment into account when assessing the total loss.

If the claimant is still unemployed at the date of the tribunal hearing then the tribunal must decide how long it will take the employee to find another job and catch up on earnings. If the employee has found a job at a lower salary, the tribunal must estimate how long it will be before he or she reaches the former earnings level. In many cases, if the employee is near normal retirement age then, with today's unemployment levels, tribunals will decide that the employee is unlikely to find other employment before retirement. This whole assessment is obviously open to conjecture though tribunals do take age, health, skills, etc into account.

Two points here to note. First, it has been held that an employee dismissed with pay in lieu of notice who starts another job during the notice period does not have his or her earnings during the time he or she was also paid in lieu included in the offsetting calculation as well as the actual payment in lieu. Second, if the original job would have come to an end for a fair reason in any case, for example the company closed down the workplace with total redundancies two months after the employee was dismissed for other reasons, then the loss will stop at the point of closure.

The employment and civil courts have agreed that self-employment may be a reasonable step, even if it increases the employee's loss and hence the damages in the short term.

For many employees the contractual pay and benefits package will include various benefits such as a car for private use, medical insurance, subsidised mortgages, etc and these will have to be taken into account in the assessment of damages or loss if the claimant is not in new employment enjoying equivalent benefits.

Company cars

The company car which can be used for private motoring is part of many managers' remuneration. Some employers who pay in lieu of notice allow the manager to continue to use the car during the payment in lieu period, which avoids the need to calculate the value of the private use. Tribunals and civil courts have adopted a variety of methods of assessing this value which may be complicated by factors like whether free petrol is also part of the package, if the employee contributes to the benefit in any way and the ratio of business to private mileage. It is generally accepted that the Inland Revenue's tax scales for the private use of cars and petrol are not intended to reflect their true value and therefore these are not used in the calculation of loss. One approach is to take the costs of running a car, which are published annually by the AA and the RAC, and apportion these between private and business mileage. Another way is to take the difference between the purchase price of a new car and the resale value at the end of the calculation period. However, this method overestimates the benefit by including compensation for depreciation which is normally borne by the employer.

If the car is being bought on hire purchase by the employer and would have been eventually owned by the employee, then the loss can be calculated on the basis of unpaid instalments, in proportion to take account of business and private use.

Accommodation

Subsidised living accommodation is usually valued on either its true rent or the rent of comparable accommodation, actual or notional.

Mortgage subsidies and other loans are valued at the difference between the cost to the employee of the loan and the cost on the open market. Medical and other insurance is valued at the cost of providing equivalent benefits for the period in question. Other examples of lost contractual benefits, the loss of which have been valued by the courts, are share options and benefits in kind. In one case a farm manager was compensated for his usual perk of a large number of eggs and 42 pints of milk a week.

There are examples of employees being awarded loss where their holiday entitlement with their new employer is service-related. The cost of buying meals instead of eating in a subsidised canteen has also been included. Other successful claims have covered the cost of moving out of company-owned accommodation, the costs of setting up in business as self-employed, the costs of finding a new job, i.e. making applications and going to interviews, unless these are borne by the new employer. In the case of three Mothercare account executives, compensation awarded included the extra costs of heating, lighting and food consumed while they were unemployed at home after being unfairly dismissed.

Pensions

The calculation of pension loss is extremely complex. The Government Actuary prepared a paper in 1981 outlining a suggested method but it should be noted that tribunals are not bound to use this method but must consider whether the employee is likely to join a compatible scheme with another employer and the likelihood of him or her leaving that employer before retirement.

Consultation

The Industrial Relations Code of Practice 1972 recommends that if unions are recognised for collective bargaining purposes management should:

- maintain jointly with the union effective arrangements for negotiation, consultation and communication and for settling grievances and disputes;
- take all reasonable steps to ensure that managers observe agreements and use agreed procedure;
- make clear to employees that it welcomes their membership of an appropriate union and their participation in union activities.

Continuous employment

To qualify for a number of rights under employment legislation an employee must have been 'continuously employed' by the employer, or an associated employer, for a minimum period. For example a full time employee who joined a company on or after 1 June 1985 must have two years' service before he can claim unfair dismissal.

Full-time is defined under the legislation as employed under a contract of employment which specifies a normal working week of 16 hours or more even if on some occasions the employee may have actually worked less than 16 hours.

If a full-time employee agreed to a change to the contract so that the normal working week is less than 16 hours but still 8 hours or more, this will not break continuous employment unless the period of fewer hours exceeds 26 weeks.

Part-time employees are covered by the legislation providing their contracts specify a normal working week of at least 8 hours and they have been employed by the employer or an associated employer for a minimum of five years.

Broken periods

A period of employment can be broken for some reasons and yet missing weeks still count towards continuous employment. These reasons are:

- sickness or injury, providing the person returns to work within 26 weeks of the contract ending;
- pregnancy or confinement, providing the woman returns to work within 26 weeks of the contract ending, unless she is entitled to statutory maternity leave when different time limits apply;
- a temporary cessation of work, for example due to a fire at the place of work, even if the employee works for someone else in the meantime: the test is that the period of absence is short in duration in comparison with the total period of employment;
- absence from work in circumstances such that by custom or arrangement the employee is regarded as continuing in the employment of the employer for all or any purposes — examples could be attendance at a prolonged training course or a temporary secondment to another employer. However the arrangement must be made or the custom exist before the previous contract ended;
- if an employee is locked out, the period of lock-out counts towards continuous service. However, if an employee has been on strike, the periods of service before and after the strike count towards continuous service but not the actual weeks when the strike took place.

Retention of rights

When an employee has qualified for a redundancy payment by completing the two years' continuous employment, that qualification is retained if an employee then becomes part-time, providing the contract is for 8 hours or more a week. If the contract is for less than 8 hours the qualification is retained, provided the employee actually works 16 or more hours a week.

The same rules apply to entitlement to statutory notice. For example, a woman works under contract for 20 hours a week for two years and then her contract is varied so she works for 10 hours a week for another two years before being made redundant. Her redundancy pay will be based on four years' service and she will be entitled to four weeks' statutory notice. If an employee is paid a redundancy payment and then either re-engaged by the employer or by the new owner of the business and subsequently made redundant again the first period of employment does not count when calculating the second redundancy payment. However, if the second period of employment followed a complaint of unfair dismissal and an order or agreement to re-engage or reinstate the employee, the employee can repay the redundancy payment and all service will be reckoned as continuous before the dismissal, the intervening period and the period following re-engagement.

Service is continuous if:

- an employee becomes employed by an associated employer;
- a trade or business is transferred from one person to another as a going concern (see Transfer of Undertakings Regulations);
- the employer dies and the employee is hired by the personal representatives or trustees of the deceased employer;
- there is a change in the partners, personal representatives or trustees who employ the employee.

Contracts of employment

There is no legal requirement that employees in general should have written contracts of employment. There are certain exceptions, for example for apprentices, fishermen and the crews of merchant ships. However, every full-time employee does have the right to a written statement of *Particulars of Employment* which must be issued within 13 weeks of the employee joining the organisation. An advertisement for a vacancy is not part of an employment contract, but verbal statements made when the post is offered to a candidate, for example, 'you will get a salary increase at the end of three months', are part of the contract. The letter offering a post or confirming an appointment and any documents detailing terms and conditions which are sent with it are the fundamental terms of a contract of employment.

An offer of a job can be withdrawn at any time before the potential employee accepts and the revocation takes effect when it reaches him. However, if his acceptance crosses in the post then a contract has been created and notice, or more practically, payment in lieu of notice, is due to him. An employer can make an offer with time limits after which the offer lapses.

A candidate's acceptance can be express — verbally or in writing — or it can be implied by his conduct in turning up on the due date and starting the job.

Comprehensive written contracts are comparatively rare particularly for blue collar workers, although the use of documents which are incorporated into the contract of employment itself by reference to them in appointment letters, job descriptions and written statements of particulars is frequently found. Employee handbooks usually set out terms and conditions, disciplinary and grievance procedures, works rules and other contractual obligations and the fact that the employee handbook is part of the contract should be stated in the appointment letter, starting form or whatever is used to confirm the job offer.

Implied terms

Contracts of employment include implied terms which are not spelt out in the individual contract but which are essential to the contract and its performance. For example, the employer has an obligation to look after the safety, health and welfare of his employees; the employee has at common law an obligation to give loyal service, and during his working hours, to work solely for the employer and his interests. The employee has a duty to protect the employer's property, including trade secrets, lists of customers and secret processes. An exception to implied terms arises in respect of so-called 'voluntary duties'. These may meet the test of implied terms but the general principle is that a voluntary duty is one that the employee can choose to undertake or not as he pleases; there is no contractual obligation. In the absence of this obligation it is not possible to discipline an employee who refuses to do what he is asked as there is no power to order him to do it. Terms implied by custom and practice also form part of the contract but the custom must be proved to be a contractual obligation for the courts to interpret it as such. For example, the fact that an employee regularly works overtime on a particular day or days is not enough to establish overtime working as contractual unless other tests are satisfied.

Variations

A contractual term may be varied either by the employees themselves agreeing to the change or by agreement with the union which represents them. An employee's acceptance can be express or implied by his conduct, that is, he works under the new terms without complaint. Where the change results from a collective agreement this will bind the employee, providing the contract refers to such agreements even though the particular employee is not a union member.

Fixed-term contracts

Fixed-term contracts are those made for a specific stated term either fixed in advance or which can be established in advance by relevant circumstances, for example the end of a school term, which can be identified with some precise date in the future. It is not a contract for a specific task which will end when it is completed on some unspecified date. A contract which has some provision in it for its renewal is not a fixed-term contract. Fixed-term contracts 'endure for a maximum definite period, not for a stated minimum period with provision for further extensions'. The right to sue for unfair dismissal does not apply to fixed-term contracts of one year or more where the dismissal consists only of the expiry of the contract without its renewal, providing the employee has previously agreed in writing to waive his right to complain of unfair dismissal.

Employees engaged on fixed-term contracts of two years or more can also waive their right to a redundancy payment on expiry of the contract.

There is some uncertainty about the validity in law of an exclusion clause included in the last of a series of fixed-term contracts of less than one year but with a combined duration exceeding two years.

Whether a new fixed-term contract entered into either before or after the expiry of the previous contract but with a break between will entitle the employee to build up continuous employment for statutory employment protection purposes depends on whether the gap between the two contracts is attributable to a temporary cessation of work.

Frustration of contracts

The concept of the frustration of a contract may sometimes, but very rarely, operate when an employee is unable to work as required by his contract because of circumstances beyond his control and which could not have been anticipated. Therefore the employment ends without there having been either a resignation or a dismissal as such. However, cases of frustration are rare and it is very unwise for an employer to rely on frustration as an excuse for getting rid of an employee. It has been established in the courts that a prison sentence cannot frustrate a contract because the concept requires that there is no fault by either party, and a custodial sentence is hardly due to something which is beyond the control of the employee. Deliberate conduct which leads to impossibility of performance is technically a repudiation of the contract and the employer must take disciplinary action, probably dismissal, because if he does not, he will be held as allowing the contract to continue.

Illegal contracts

The courts will not enforce contracts entered into for purposes which are either forbidden by law or which, although not expressly forbidden, are immoral. If the employee contracts to do a criminal act, such as to not declare income for tax purposes or for an immoral purpose, for example to procure and pay prostitutes, his contract is not enforceable.

In practice the situation is less clear where the contract is not primarily illegal but there is an element of illegality. In a leading case on this issue *Coral Leisure Group* v *Barnett* 1981, the Employment Appeals Tribunal said:

> The question to be answered is whether any taint of illegality affecting part of a contract necessarily renders the whole contract unenforceable by a party who knew of the illegality. In our judgement a distinction has to be drawn between (a) cases in which there is a contractual obligation to do an act which is unlawful, and (b) cases where the contractual obligations are capable of being performed lawfully and were initially intended so to be performed, but which have in fact been performed by unlawful means. As to category (a), the answer to the question depends on what is often called the rules of severance, i.e. how far is it possible to separate the tainted contractual obligations from the untainted? As to category (b), the question is whether the doing of an unlawful act by a party to the contract precludes his further enforcement of that contract.

The knowledge by the employer and/or the employee of the illegality is important. For example, if the employer does not declare cash payments to the Inland Revenue but the employee is unaware of this, he can enforce his statutory rights but the employer cannot. From the employee's point of view the question is not whether he ought to have known but whether he did in fact know. When undercover payments come to the notice of the employment courts they may direct that the papers on the case are sent to the Inland Revenue.

Unfair contracts

The Unfair Contracts Terms Act prevents unfair or unreasonable exclusion clauses and other terms (including the limitation of liability for breach of contract or for negligence) in contracts and notices used in the course of business. For example, an employer cannot avoid all liability if an employee damages someone's car in the company car park by simply putting up a notice to that effect. He would have to show that reasonable steps to prevent damage had been taken.

The Act provides that any term in an employment contract which excludes liability for negligence resulting in death or personal injury is void. Liability for other losses or damage cannot be excluded or restricted except in so far as such a clause is reasonable.

It is for the person claiming that a contract term or notice is reasonable to prove it.

Court of Appeal

The next level of appeal in England and Wales beyond the Employment Appeal

Tribunal is the Court of Appeal. The constitution of the Court of Appeal when deciding such matters is not in any way changed for the purposes of dealing with employment appeals. The judges of the Court of Appeal decide any type of appeal which is proper should be referred to them. Many of the judgments of the Court of Appeal have been of great importance as guidelines to industrial tribunals when deciding cases brought under the employment protection and discrimination legislation.

In Scotland the next level of appeal beyond the Employment Appeal Tribunal is the Court of Session Inner House. The role of that Court in dealing with such appeals is similar to that of the Court of Appeal in England and Wales.

Disabled employees

The Disabled Persons (Employment) Acts 1944 and 1958 established a voluntary register of disabled people. The main eligibility conditions for registering as disabled are that the applicant:

- is substantially handicapped in getting and keeping employment or work on his/her own account;
- has a disability which is likely to last for at least 12 months;
- must want some kind of paid employment or work on his/her own account;
- must have reasonable prospects of obtaining and keeping employment or work on his/her own account;
- must ordinarily be resident in Great Britain.

Medical evidence is almost always required.

The Acts place certain duties and obligations on employers with 20 or more workers, relating to the employment of registered disabled. Under the quota scheme these employers have a duty to employ disabled workers as 3 per cent of their total workforce. It is not an offence to be below quota but if the employer has less than 3 per cent he has a duty to take on suitable disabled persons when a vacancy arises and he must obtain a permit if he wants to engage any one other than a disabled person.

An employer must not dismiss a disabled person without reasonable cause if this would bring the numbers retained below quota. Bulk permits can be issued to authorise the engagement of a specified number of workers over a period of six months on the understanding that the vacancies will be notified to the local job centre and applications from registered disabled will be sympathetically considered.

Under the designated employments scheme of the 1944 Act the occupations of car park attendant and passenger electric lift attendant are reserved for registered disabled persons but these jobs do not count towards the quota. Employing disabled persons who are not registered does not count towards meeting the quota either.

Employers are required to keep records of all employees with starting and finishing dates; registered disabled employees; employees employed under a permit and those in designated employment. These records must be available for inspection by officials authorised by the Manpower Services Commission. Penalties for failure to comply with some of these provisions range up to a fine of £100 or three months' imprisonment. The directors' report of companies who employed on average 250 or more employees in the financial year to which the report relates must contain a statement describing the policy which applied in that financial year for giving full and fair consideration to disabled people applying for jobs, having regard to their particular aptitudes and abilities.

Disclosure

The disclosure to employees and their representatives of information about their company's future developments, trading position and prospects, and financial and other economic factors is seen as an essential part of contemporary industrial relations. The government is concerned that it should be achieved through agreements and arrangements established voluntarily, believing that these are more effective, and more desirable, than legislation compelling the disclosure of information covering a wide range of specified topics.

Two existing provisions of employment law require the disclosure of information in limited circumstances:

- statements to be included in the annual directors' reports of larger companies; and
- the disclosure of information to trade unions for collective bargaining purposes.

The directors' reports of companies employing more than 250 must include a statement describing action taken during the financial year to introduce, maintain or develop arrangements aimed at, *inter alia*:

- providing employees systematically with information on matters of concern to them as employees;
- consulting employees or their representatives regularly;
- achieving a common awareness on the part of all employees of the financial and economic factors affecting the performance of the company.

Legislation imposes a general duty on employers to disclose information to the unions they recognise for collective bargaining purposes. It gives to an independent trade union recognised by an employer for collective bargaining purposes the right to complain to the Central Arbitration Committee that the employer has failed to supply relevant information. If the CAC finds a complaint to be well-founded, it can make a declaration to that effect specifying the information in respect of which the employer's failure has occurred. If that information is still not provided, the CAC can award specific terms and conditions which will become part of the employees' contracts of employment from a date given in that further award.

Although the provision for the disclosure in directors' reports of the information mentioned above says nothing about the disclosure of information for collective bargaining purposes, the duty imposed by it would be upheld by the CAC if, for example, a company refused to disclose information about financial and economic factors which the union could show was relevant to its negotiations with management.

Equal Pay Act

There are four situations where equality of pay and other contractual terms apply:

- if a man and woman are employed on 'like work' — that is the same work, or work of a broadly similar nature where any differences between what they do are not of practical importance in relation to terms and conditions of employment;
- if the male and female jobs have been rated equally under a job evaluation study which has considered the demands made on them under such headings as skill, effort and decision;
- if the jobs would have been rated equally but one has been given fewer points for the same level of a particular factor, such as effort, skill or decision-making, than the other;
- if the woman does work, which in terms of the demands made upon her under such headings as skill, effort and decision, is of equal value to that of a man in the same employment.

The man or woman must be 'in the same employment' which includes employment at a different establishment or associated employer, providing there are common terms and conditions generally or for employees of the relevant classes. A woman may make a comparison with a man who was employed prior to her period of employment and who did equal work for the employer.

An employer may be able to show that the variation in pay between the man and the woman is due to a *material factor* which is not the difference of sex. Such a factor might include length of service or particular personal skills.

Like work

Under the Act:

A woman is to be regarded as employed on like work with men if, but only if, her work and theirs is of the same broadly similar nature, and the differences (if any) between the things she does and the things they do are not of practical importance in relation to terms and conditions of employment; and accordingly in comparing her work with theirs regard shall be had to the frequency or otherwise with which any such differences occur in practice as well as to the nature and extent of the differences.

With an equal claim the claimant must show that her work is of equal value to that of the man she is comparing herself with, not of greater or less value.

A claim based on job evaluation depends on whether there has been a true job evaluation study giving the jobs of man and woman equal value:

in terms of the demand made on a worker under various headings (for instance effort, skill, decision), in a study undertaken with a view to evaluating in those terms the jobs to be done by all or any of the employees in an undertaking or group of undertakings, or would have been given an equal value but for the evaluation being made on a system setting different values for men and women on the same demand under any heading.

The Equal Pay Act implies that the onus is on the employee to specify the difference between her treatment, or her contract, and that of the man and:

- identify the man whom the comparison is with and show that he is or was with the same employer;
- show that her work is like or broadly similar to his; or
- show that her work and his were rated equally under a job evaluation scheme; or
- if there is no job evaluation scheme, show that her work and his are of equal value.

The claim to a tribunal can be made either during employment or up to six months after the termination of the job to which the claim relates. Claims for backpay etc., cannot be backdated to more than two years before the date of the claim to the tribunal.

Job evaluation

A claim based on job evaluation can be made where either:

- the male and female jobs have been rated equally through job evaluation which has taken into account such factors as effort, skill, decision-making, etc.;
- the jobs would have been rated equal but the woman's job has been given fewer points for the same levels of effort, skill, decision-making than the man's.

The woman does not have to compare her work with the man's as the job evaluation exercise will have done this.

Health and safety

The regulations governing health and safety in offices, shops and factories are enforced by the Health and Safety Executive (1 Chepstow Place, London W2) through its inspectors. Requirements include:

- at least 40 square feet of space per person (or 400 cubic feet when the ceiling is below 10 feet);
- weekly cleaning;
- adequate heating, lighting and ventilation;
- adequate toilet and washing facilities;
- first aid box;
- a poster (OSR 9) or equivalent booklet (OSR 9B) must be on display.

The Fire Regulations Act 1971 requires means of escape in case of fire; and for certification when the number of workers is more than 20 (or more than 10 elsewhere than on the ground floor).

Particulars of employment

A written statement of particulars of employment must be given to an employee not later than 13 weeks from the date the employee's employment began where the employee's contract requires him normally to work at least 16 hours a week.

Part-timers whose contracts require them to work at least 8 hours a week are eligible for a written statement once they have completed five years' continuous service. There is no need to give a new statement to an employee who leaves and comes back on the same terms, providing he returns within 6 months.

The employee must be informed of any change in the information contained in the statement within one month of the change occurring. This can be done by either:

- giving a note of the change to each employee; or
- telling him in the original statement that changes will be notified by some other way, for example by being posted on notice boards or by entry into some reasonably accessible document.

The written statement does not have to include the detail under each heading, providing this is reasonably accessible elsewhere, for example in collective agreements or works rules.

If the employee has a formal written contract, then provided it covers the information required in a written statement, there is no requirement for a separate statement.

It is common practice to require employees to sign written statements but this is of little value apart from indicating that the employee has received his statement, because the statement itself does not establish contractual terms unless it was issued as part of the offer of employment and the employee therefore has accepted the statement in accepting the offer. Amending the written statement alone will not amend the contract.

Right to complain

If the employee is not given a statement within 13 weeks he or she can complain to an industrial tribunal who can decide what terms should have been in the statement in order to comply with the Act. If the employee has been given a statement but there is a query about the particulars which ought to have been included or referred to, the employee or the employer can ask a tribunal to adjudicate with two exceptions:

- where the dispute is about the accuracy of the amount stated in a written pay statement;
- on the question of whether the employment is contracted in or out under the Social Security Pensions Act 1975.

Content

The minimum details specified for inclusion in a written statement are:

- the names of the employee and the employer;
- the date when the employment began;
- the date on which the employee's period of continuous employment began, taking into account any employment with a previous employer which counts towards that period;
- the scale, rate or method of calculating remuneration (including overtime pay, bonus payments, etc);
- the intervals at which remuneration is paid;
- any terms and conditions relating to hours of work (including normal working hours and contractual overtime);
- any terms and conditions relating to holiday entitlement (including public holidays) and holiday pay, including any entitlement to accrued holiday pay on the termination of employment;
- any terms and conditions relating to sick leave, absence through injury, and sick pay;
- any terms and conditions relating to pensions and pension schemes (except where the employee's pension rights depend on the terms of a pension scheme established in consequence of an Act of Parliament and the employer is required by such a provision to give information to new employees about their pension rights);
- the length of notice which the employee is obliged to give and entitled to receive to determine his contract of employment;
- the title of the job which the employee is employed to do;
- any disciplinary rules applicable to the employee which must specify (except in respect of procedures relating to health and safety at work), by description or otherwise:

(a)   the person to whom the employee can apply if he is dissatisfied with any disciplinary decision relating to him; and

(b)   a person to whom the employee can apply for the purpose of seeking redress of any grievance relating to his employment, — and how such applications should be made, and, if there are further steps in the procedures, giving an explanation of those steps or referring an employee to an accessible document which contains this information;

- whether a contracting-out certificate issued under the Social Security Pensions Act 1975 is in force for the employment to which the written statement applies.

Picketing

Picketing is lawful if a person in contemplation or furtherance of a trade dispute attends:

- at or near his own place of work; or
- if he is an official of a trade union, at or near the place of work of a member of that union whom he is accompanying and whom he represents;

for the purpose only of peacefully obtaining or communicating information, or peacefully persuading any person to work or abstain from working.

The essential ingredients are that:

- the picketing must be in contemplation or furtherance of a trade dispute; and
- the ways in which the picketing is conducted must be peaceful.

If a person works or normally works:

- otherwise than at any one place; or
- at a place which is so located that attendance there for picketing is impracticable;

he can peacefully picket at any premises of his employer from which he works or from which his work is administered. An employee who works at only one place, therefore, can only lawfully picket there and nowhere else, such as at his employer's administrative headquarters, while an employee who works at two or more places is free to picket lawfully at the company's administrative headquarters.

The statutory right to picket peacefully does not extend to a 'right to attend on land against the will of its owner (or of the person to whom the owner has granted exclusive occupation), nor does it affect the operation of any byelaws by which the use and operation of that land is regulated'. An employer is, therefore, entitled to apply for a court order to restrain persons, their organisers, and/or their unions from picketing within the limits of his property.

Liability of unions

When picketing occurs, the immunity from actions for civil breach (i.e. matters which are actionable in tort in England and Wales) in contemplation or furtherance of a trade dispute, only applies when the picketing is lawful. This means that, when unlawful picketing occurs (e.g. secondary picketing), it is open to anyone suffering damage or loss to take civil action against named pickets, named organisers of them and/or, if he can show that the unlawful picketing was authorised or endorsed by a responsible person, the union on whose behalf, or in whose name, the picketing was authorised or endorsed. Union funds are, therefore, at risk if their 'responsible persons' authorise or endorse unlawful picketing which, for example, interferes with the performance of contracts.

Proceedings for damages

Not only employers can bring proceedings against unions for unlawful picketing; an individual employee of an organisation which is being unlawfully picketed may, for example, be able to sue the union in whose name the picketing has been authorised or endorsed, if he can show that:

- the picketing was unlawful;
- it was not authorised or endorsed by a responsible person;
- he was prevented from performing a primary obligation under his contract of employment (e.g. working), or was being unreasonably harassed in the exercise of his right to work; and
- he has suffered loss or damage because of it.

To succeed with such an action the employee would also have to show that he was available and ready to perform his full duties. This would probably mean crossing the picket line as the first step.

Intimidation

To an individual worker who wants to cross a picket line and is faced with what to him or to her may look like aggressive pickets, the thought that the pickets are only lawfully entitled to indulge in the peaceful communication of information or the peaceful persuasion of the worker, may not be the one foremost in his or her mind. This is particularly likely to be so where, as alleged in one case, the pickets were carrying sledgehammers and, apart from making threats involving personal safety, made it clear that a person crossing the picket line without the union's authority could lose his union card and hence, as a union membership agreement with that union existed in his firm, his job.

There is no general rule by which intimidation by pickets can be objectively assessed. All that can be said is that intimidation is unlawful, but what constitutes intimidation will depend on the facts of any particular instance when it is alleged. Where the question of whether intimidation occurs or not arises, the individual who is intimidated is in the best position to decide whether someone is inspiring fear in him, but this is not the sole basis on which intimidation can be assessed: a witness to the actions may be in a good position to support an allegation of intimidation. However, it is one thing to identify certain picketing as intimidatory, but quite another to do anything about it.

Variations of intimidation

Intimidation is only one of the criminal offences which non-peaceful picketing may involve. Variations of intimidation, and other criminal offences, which can occur include any action which is likely to lead to a breach of the peace, and particularly:

(a) obstructing a police officer in the execution of his duty;
(b) obstruction of the highway or the entrance to premises;
(c) damage to property;
(d) possession of an offensive weapon;
(e) use of violence to, or intimidation of, a person or his wife or children, or injury to his property;
(f) persistently following a person about from place to place;
(g) hiding any tools, clothes or other property owned or used by a person, or depriving him of, or hindering him in, the use thereof;
(h) watching or besetting the house or other place where a person resides, or works, or carries on business, or happens to be, or the approach to such house or place:
(i) following a person with two or more other persons in a disorderly manner in or through any street or road.

Racial equality, Commission for

The Commission for Racial Equality (CRE) was set up under the Race Relations Act 1976. Its statutory duties are to work towards the elimination of discrimination and to promote equality of opportunity and good relations between different racial groups generally. It is also charged with keeping the working of the Act under review and proposing amendments.

The Commission may:

- issue Codes of Practice;
- set up formal investigations into alleged discrimination;
- issue non discrimination notices following an investigation;

- obtain a county court injunction if a non discrimination notice is not complied with within 5 years.

The Commission will provide guidance and assistance to individuals complaining of discrimination to an industrial tribunal.

Redundancy

An employee may be dismissed as redundant if:

- his employer ceases to carry on the business which employs him;
- his employer closes down the business at the site where he works;
- his employer transfers the business from the site where he works to another location;
- his employer needs fewer employees to do his particular kind of work;
- his employer needs fewer employees to do his particular kind of work at the place where he works.

The basic test of redundancy is whether an employer now needs fewer employees, either across the company or at a particular site.

True redundancy is a fair reason for dismissal but there are a number of circumstances in which an employee made redundant can sue for unfair dismissal.

Dismissal for redundancy will be unfair if it can be shown that there were other employees in similar positions who were not dismissed and that:

- the employee was selected because he took part in union activities at an appropriate time or because he was/was not a member of a trade union. (There are additional complications where a closed shop is in force); or
- the employee was selected in breach of a customary or agreed selection procedure and there were no special reasons which justified a departure from it.

The statutory unit of selection is 'the same undertaking'. In cases brought before the employment courts, tribunals have had to decide whether 'undertaking' means the whole of an employer's business or particular departments or sections. For example, if employees are selected for redundancy on the basis of last in first out, should this be across the site or section by section? Much depends on the particular circumstances. On the whole, the less skilled the employee, the wider the field which normally will form the unit of selection within a site. Where managerial jobs are carried out on a number of sites, the unit of selection could be company wide, for example between sales managers with different areas.

Comparisons can only be with similar positions and generally tribunals have accepted that employees who are interchangeable in their skills can be held to be employed in similar positions.

Suitable alternative employment

If an employer withdraws a notice of redundancy or offers 'suitable alternative employment' before the date the notice expires, and this employment will begin not more than four weeks after that date, an employee will normally lose his entitlement to statutory redundancy pay if he refuses such an offer without reasonable cause. Where such alternative employment is offered, the offer must be set out in sufficient detail to show where the new employment differs from the old and must give all major terms. The employee has a right to a trial period of four weeks in the new job or an agreed longer period if retraining is involved. If he decides in that time that the job is not suitable, he can leave and claim a redundancy payment. If the employer insists that the new work is suitable, the employee may have to claim payment through an industrial tribunal.

Alternative employment

In a redundancy situation an employer has a duty to take reasonable steps to look for other employment within the company for redundant employees. In broad terms, any other work which the employee might reasonably do should be offered unless the offer would be derogatory, for example if a substantial demotion is involved, or if the employer already has good reason to believe that the employee would not accept it. If the employer fails to take reasonable steps to look for other employment, or fails to offer other employment which is available, this can make dismissal for redundancy unfair.

Rights to consultation

Employers who recognise independent trade unions for collective bargaining must consult them about proposed redundancies affecting the class of employee for whom the union is recognised, whether the employees actually affected are union members or not.

Consultation must take place at the earliest opportunity but no later than:

- where the employer is proposing to dismiss as redundant 100 or more employees at one establishment within a period of 90 days or less — at least 90 days before the first dismissal takes effect.
- where the employer is proposing to dismiss as redundant 10 or more employees at one establishment within a period of 30 days or less — at least 30 days before the first dismissal takes effect.

If fewer than 10 employees are involved, there is no minimum time period but the requirement to consult at the earliest possible opportunity is still there. Individuals also have the right to be consulted about their redundancy.

Essential Facts for Managers

The reasons for the redundancies and why a particular employee has been selected should be explained and information given about any alternative employment. An employee may be able successfully to claim unfair redundancy if he has not been properly consulted and can show that if proper consultation had taken place the outcome would have been different.

Notice rights

For an employee working 16 hours or more a week, the following statutory provisions for minimum notice apply:

The employer must give:

- one week's notice after four weeks' service;
- two weeks' notice after two years' service and then an additional week's notice for each year's service up to a maximum of twelve weeks' notice for twelve years' service.

Going to an industrial tribunal

If an employee feels his redundancy has been unfairly handled by his employer he can make a claim to an industrial tribunal. There are minimum service requirements for bringing a claim:

- one year for employees who work at least 16 hours a week for an employer of 21 or more employees;
- two years for employees who work at least 16 hours a week for an employer who has not employed more than 20 employees at any time during that 2 years, including any in associated companies;
- five years for employees who work at least 8 hours a week but less than 16.

There is no service requirement if an employee claims unfair dismissal on the grounds of sex, race, membership or non-membership of a trade union.

Normally a claim must be brought within 3 months of the last day worked for the employer.

Redundancy pay

An employee under the age of 65 in the case of a man, or 60 in the case of a woman, who has been continuously employed for two years while over the age of 18 and who is dismissed by his employer because of redundancy is entitled to a lump sum redundancy payment related to his age, length of continuous employment and weekly pay and calculated as prescribed in the Employment Protection (Consolidation) Act 1978.

The amount of this payment is:

(a) one-and-a-half weeks' pay for each complete year of employment consisting wholly of weeks in which the employee was not below the age of 41;
(b) one week's pay for each complete year of employment not falling within (a) and consisting wholly of weeks in which the employee was not below the age of 22; and
(c) half a week's pay for each complete year of employment not falling within either (a) or (b).

Employment before age 18 is not taken into account, and the maximum length of employment brought into account at all ages is 20 years.

An employee's right to a redundancy payment may be extinguished, or the amount of the payment reduced, if the employee has a right to a pension or gratuity or superannuation allowance. If an employee becomes redundant after the attainment of the age of 64 in the case of a man, or 59 in the case of a woman, the redundancy payment is reduced by one-twelfth for each complete month over that age.

A redundancy rebate of 41 per cent of the redundancy payment made by an employer, and for which he was liable, may be made to him out of the Redundancy Fund. Payment may be made direct from the Fund to an employee who is entitled to a redundancy payment but is unable to obtain it from his employer.

Rehabilitation of offenders

The Act relates to terms of imprisonment of up to two and a half years and provides that following a specific period of rehabilitation, i.e. when there were no convictions, the offence is treated as 'spent' for the purpose of employment, with the exception of certain occupations. The periods of rehabilitation vary from six months for an absolute discharge to ten years for sentences of between six months and two and a half years.

The employer cannot treat a spent conviction 'as a proper ground for dismissing or excluding a person from any office, profession, occupation or employment, or for prejudicing him in any way in any occupation or employment'.

Therefore, a job applicant need not declare a spent conviction on an application form; the discovery by the employer of a conviction would not be grounds for dismissal if at the time of dismissal the conviction was spent.

Excluded occupations include certain professions e.g. medical, legal, dentists, vets, opticians, pharmaceutical chemists, teachers in Scotland.

If an employer disclosed a spent conviction when giving a reference, there is a danger that this could be considered as malicious and he could be sued for libel. The normal defence to libel that the statement was true, even if given with malice, would not apply in this case.

Sex discrimination

The Equal Pay Act 1970 and the Sex Discrimination Act 1975 are complementary. The SDA prohibits direct and indirect sex discrimination against men or women in selection for appointment, promotion, transfer or training. The EPA is designed to prevent discrimination against men or women in their contracts of employment, including pay.

References to discrimination against women in this entry must be read as applying equally to discrimination against men or against married persons unless otherwise stated.

The areas covered by the two Acts are summarised below.

- The Equal Pay Act applies to:
  - (a) remuneration under contracts of employment;
  - (b) complaints that less favourable treatment is being applied under the contracts of employment of employees of the opposite sex at the same establishment who are, or have been, doing the same or broadly similar work, or whose posts have job-evaluated equally or — where job evaluation has not been carried out — who are doing work of equal value to a person of the opposite sex in the same employment.
- The Sex Discrimination Act applies to:
  - (a) less favourable treatment which is not covered by a contract of employment, either directly under the Act or through the terms of the Equal Pay Act;
  - (b) complaints about matters contained in a contract of employment, but where comparisons are being made with employees who are not doing the same or broadly similar work;
  - (c) in the more hypothetical case where, although a matter is covered by the employee's contract of employment, the allegation is that a member of the other sex would be treated more favourably in similar circumstances, but is not being so treated at the time of complaint.

Excluded employees

These employments are excluded from the provisions of the Acts:

- wholly or mainly outside Great Britain;
- aboard a ship registered in Great Britain where the employee works wholly outside Great Britain;
- wholly outside Great Britain on an aircraft or hovercraft registered in the United Kingdom and operated by a person who has his principal place of business, or is ordinarily resident, in Great Britain;
- in a private household;

- in a firm, including with any associated employer, with not more than five employees, including part-time employees, but excluding any employees employed in a private household. This exclusion is limited by the total number of the employer's employers, not by the number of employees in any one establishment, and it applies only to the Sex Discrimination Act.
- service in the Navy, Army or Air Force or in the Women's Services, and (but not for the Equal Pay Act) employment in support of the armed forces.

Employers can discriminate in the following circumstances without contravening the Acts.

- In the provision of special rights for women in respect of their pregnancy and confinement.
- With regard to death or retirement (e.g. in respect of the age of retirement, terms of a pension scheme, etc). For the purposes of the Act, retirement includes retirement whether voluntary or not, on grounds of age, length of service or incapacity. However, the EPA applies to equal access under contracts of employment to membership of occupational pension schemes on terms which are the same for both men and women with regard to age and length of service and whether membership is voluntary or compulsory.
- With regard to terms and conditions of a woman's employment which are in any respect affected by compliance with the law regulating the employment of women.

The two Acts apply to part-time employees. No minimum period of employment with the employer is required under those Acts for part-time or full-time employees before such an employee can become eligible to exercise his or her rights.

The Acts apply to persons of any age. The right to make a claim to an industrial tribunal does not cease at the normal retiring age or the age of 65 for men, 60 for women.

The Sex Discrimination Act will not apply to certain Acts passed before 1975 and to discriminatory practices which are the result of an employer complying with laws regulating the employment of women, for example the Factories Act of 1961 or when giving women special treatment in connection with pregnancy or childbirth.

Direct discrimination

Defined as discrimination against:

- anyone, if, on the ground of that person's sex, another person treats him or her less favourably then he treats or would treat a person of the opposite sex; or
- a married person of either sex if, on the ground of his or her marital

status, another person treats him or her less favourably than he treats or would treat an unmarried person of the same sex.

Indirect discrimination

This may occur if a person applies:

* to a woman a requirement or condition which he applies, or would apply, equally to a man but
  (a) which is such that the proportion of women who can comply with it is considerably smaller than the proportion of men who can comply with it;
  (b) which he cannot show to be justifiable irrespective of the sex of the person to whom it is applied; and
  (c) which is to her detriment because she cannot comply with it;
* a married person of either sex a requirement or condition which he applies, or would apply, equally to an unmarried person but
  (a) which is such that the proportion of married persons who can comply with it is considerably smaller than the proportion of unmarried persons of the same sex who can comply with it; and
  (b) which he cannot show to be justifiable irrespective of the marital status of the person to whom it is applied; and
  (c) which is to that person's detriment because he cannot comply with it.

If the purpose of a requirement or condition is to exclude or otherwise penalise a person of a particular sex, then it is directly discriminatory. If this was not the purpose but the effect is discriminatory, then this is indirect discrimination.

An employee complaining of indirect discrimination must:

* establish what is the particular requirement or condition;
* show that whoever made the selection, for example, applied this condition to the complainant;
* show that a substantially smaller proportion of his sex/marital status could comply;
* show the detriment that has resulted.

No award of damages or compensation is made in the case of indirect discrimination if the discriminator can show that his actions did not have a discriminatory motive.

There is no definition of 'a substantially smaller proportion'.

Limited right to discriminate

Employers have a limited right to discriminate in certain jobs where being of a certain sex or marital status is a genuine occupational qualification. However, this applies only to recruiting, training, promoting or transferring people into these particular jobs, not to other factors such as their terms and conditions.

An employer who already has employees of the required sex or marital status cannot recruit from outside for these jobs if the existing employees are capable of doing the jobs, could be reasonably employed and there are enough of them not to cause undue inconvenience if they carried out these tasks.

Genuine occupational qualifications may apply to a job to be held by a man or woman:

- for physiological reasons excluding strength and stamina;
- for authenticity e.g. a stage role or modelling clothes;
- for reasons of privacy or decency e.g. where physical contact or using toilet facilities/undressing in the presence of members of the opposite sex is involved and they might object;
- where there is only single sex accommodation, the location of the establishment makes it impracticable for the employee to live anywhere else and it is unreasonable to expect the employer to provide separate facilities;
- jobs in single sex hospitals, prisons, etc., and it is reasonable to restrict the particular job to a person of the same sex (this would apply only to posts where there was direct contact with patients, inmates, etc);
- jobs in welfare or education or other personal services which can be best done by a person of a particular sex where legal restrictions apply, for example on women working with lead or on night shifts;
- a job which is likely to involve work abroad in a country which has laws or customs which prevent the work from being done by a particular sex;
- a job which is one of two held by a married couple.

Where a complainant to a tribunal shows that he/she is less favourably treated because of his/her sex and the employer pleads a genuine occupational qualification he must show that it exists and is reasonable.

Discrimination in selection

The SDA makes it unlawful for an employer to discriminate against a prospective or actual job applicant:

- in the arrangements he makes for determining who should be offered that employment;
- in the terms on which the employment is offered;
- by refusing or deliberately omitting to offer an individual that employment, including deliberate omission from a shortlist on the grounds of the applicant's sex or marital status. The only exception would be where there is a genuine occupational qualification.

Essential Facts for Managers

In the case of existing employees it is unlawful to discriminate:

- in opportunities for promotion, transfer or training, or any other benefits, facilities or services;
- by dismissing an individual or by subjecting him or her to any other detriment.

Discrimination in advertising

It is unlawful to publish an advertisement which indicates an intention to discriminate against applications of a particular sex or marital status, except where there is a genuine occupational qualification.

The publisher of the advertisement is not liable if he can show that he has relied on a statement by the advertiser that the advertisement is not unlawful.

Only the Equal Opportunities Commission, not individuals, can bring a complaint of discriminatory advertising.

It is unlawful for an employer to give instructions to some outside agency to the effect that persons of a particular sex or marital status will be preferred.

Pressures to discriminate

It is unlawful for anyone to require a subordinate to do something which is unlawful under the SDA. Only the EOC can bring a case under this section except where the subordinate is then penalised for refusing to carry out the order when he or she can then claim discrimination.

Sexual harassment is not dealt with directly by the SDA. However, if an employee was demoted, for example because she objected to behaviour which could be considered to constitute sexual harassment, she could make a complaint.

Positive action

The SDA allows limited positive discrimination in respect of training in certain conditions.

- Training bodies may provide training for women only or men only where there have been no, or proportionally fewer, employees of that sex in Great Britain or in a particular area engaged on the work to which the training is directed.
- Employers may provide access to training facilities for members of one sex where there have been no employees of that sex doing that work, or proportionally fewer in relation to their numbers in the workforce. In these circumstances, employers may also encourage employees of the

under-represented sex to apply for training to fit them for the particular work.

Contractors' employees

It is unlawful for an employer who engages a contractor to do certain work to discriminate against the contractor's employees:

- in the terms in which he allows the employee to do the work;
- by not allowing him to do it, except where there is a genuine occupational qualification;
- in the way in which he allows him any benefits, facilities or services;
- by otherwise treating him unfavourably.

Complaints

A complaint under the SDA must be made to an industrial tribunal within three months of the date of the act to which the complaint relates. This period can be extended if a tribunal considers that this would be just and equitable. A tribunal may declare the rights of the parties; require the respondent to pay compensation up to £8,000, or recommend that he take a specific course of action. Compensation will not be awarded in a case of indirect discrimination if the respondent can show that there was no intention to discriminate.

Under the SDA, an employer is liable for the discriminatory acts of his employees. There is also a provision that anyone who knowingly aids another person to carry out a discriminatory act will be treated as if he personally did the unlawful act. It is a defence for an employer if he can show that he took reasonably practical steps to prevent his employees from committing discriminatory acts. Therefore, co-ordinated procedures to prevent these occurring, for example when advertising or promoting, are essential.

The questionnaire procedure

There is a special procedure available under the SDA by which an employee who alleges that the employer has unlawfully discriminated can question the employer using a form — SD 74 — available from the EOC or the local offices of the Department of Employment. The form is used to help the employee to decide whether to institute proceedings against the employer and may be used in evidence at the tribunal provided the form used was served on the employer:

- before the tribunal complaint but within 3 months of the alleged act; or
- within 21 days of the claim being made to a tribunal, or later if agreed by the tribunal.

The SD 74 form is a 12-page document and includes a good deal of information and practical guidance.

Specific offences

It is an offence for a person knowingly or recklessly to make a statement in the following circumstances, which is false or misleading. The penalty for these offences will not exceed £800.

The circumstances are:

- making a statement on which an employment agency or an education authority acts;
- knowingly aiding or assisting something which is unlawful under the Act, including publishing discriminatory advertisements;
- bringing pressure on another person to commit unlawful discrimination;
- complying with a requirement to produce information to the EOC.

Statutory maternity pay

From April 6, 1987 Maternity Pay (paid by employers and refunded by the Department of Employment) and maternity allowance (paid by the DHSS) was replaced by statutory maternity pay (SMP). SMP first applied to women whose babies were due on or after June 21, 1987.

To qualify for SMP an employee must:

- have been continuously employed for at least 26 weeks continuing into the 15th week before her baby is due (known as the qualifying week);
- have average weekly earnings of not less than the lower earnings limit for the payment of National Insurance contributions which applies in the qualifying week;
- still be pregnant at the 11th week before her expected week of confinement or have been confined by that time;
- have stopped working.

SMP is payable for a maximum of 18 weeks but cannot start earlier than the 11th week before the expected week of confinement. There is, however, a degree of flexibility on the starting date. This flexibility is based on a central 'core' period of 13 weeks starting with the sixth week before the expected week of confinement. The remaining five weeks of the maximum period may be taken either all before or after this central period depending on when the employee stops working. She must, however, have given up work by the sixth week before the expected week of confinement if she is to qualify for the full 18 weeks.

There are two rates of SMP:

(a) The higher rate is 90 per cent of the employee's average weekly earnings and is payable for the first six weeks for which SMP is due.

(b) For the remainder of the period for which SMP is due, a lower rate is paid. This is reviewed each year and is published in *NI 196 Social security benefit rates and earnings rules*.

To qualify for the higher rate an employee must:

- have been employed, normally working for at least 16 hours weekly for a continuous period of two years up to and including the qualifying week; or
- have been employed, normally working for at least eight but less than 16 hours weekly for a continuous period of five years up to and including the qualifying week.

The employee

To qualify for payment of SMP an employee must give her employer at least 21 days' notice before her absence, because of pregnancy, is due to begin. She must also produce a maternity certificate form (MAT B1) issued by a doctor or midwife not earlier than 14 weeks before a baby is due.

The employee can choose to give up work because of pregnancy in any week between the 14th and seventh weeks before the expected week of confinement (both weeks inclusive) and get the full 18 weeks SMP. A week begins at midnight between Saturday and Sunday.

If an employee does not give up work until the sixth week before the expected week of confinement or later she will lose one week's SMP for each week or part of a week in which she worked. Such lost SMP will usually be at the lower rate.

An employee receiving SMP must inform her paying employer in the following instances:

- she starts to work after her baby is born for another employer by whom she was not employed during the qualifying week;
- she travels abroad outside the European Community;
- she is taken into legal custody.

An employer's liability to pay SMP ends with the week before any of the above events.

For the purposes of SMP an employee is a person whose earnings attract a liability for Employer's Class I NIC or which would if they were high enough.

The employer

An employer must tell employees how they wish to be notified of an impending absence through pregnancy. Such notification can be required in writing, if the employer so wishes. If it is not possible for an employee to give notice in person, an employer must accept notice given on her behalf.

If an employee fails to give the full 21-days' notice but does so as soon as it is reasonably practical it is for the employer to decide whether or not notice received was 'reasonably practical'. An employee denied SMP because an employer rejects her reasons for not giving proper notice may ask for the employer's reasons for refusal in writing and can apply for a formal decision by an Adjudication Officer.

Employers can recover all SMP payments (including tax and usual deductions) plus an extra amount to compensate for the NIC paid on SMP. Deductions may be made from monthly payments of NIC sent to the Collection of Taxes.

For SMP purposes, an employer is anyone liable to pay the employer's share of Class 1 NIC.

Statutory sick pay

In the absence of contractual obligation, an employer is not requried to pay wages when an employee is absent because of illness, but must give employee statutory sick pay (SSP) on behalf of the Department of Health and Social Security.

All employees over 16 and under pension age on the first day of illness are entitled to SSP after 4 consecutive calendar days of illness including Saturdays and holidays. The first 3 days of illness are 'waiting days', for which no SSP is payable. To obtain payment an employee must notify the employer within 7 days of first day of absence.

Not entitled to SSP are:

- employees whose average earnings are below the limit for National Insurance contributions;
- an employee who, within the previous 8 weeks, has been paid a State benefit (sickness benefit, invalidity benefit, severe disablement allowance, maternity allowance, and, sometimes, unemployment benefit);
- an employee who reports sick on the first day of employment (but a few minutes of work on the first day will qualify for payment);
- an employee whose period of incapacity begins while he is on strike;
- an employee who is pregnant and whose period of incapacity begins during a 'period of expected confinement';
- an employee who has been entitled in a previous employment to 28 weeks of SSP within 8 weeks of the illness in the new employment;
- an employee who is outside the European Community on the first day of incapacity. The United Kingdom, as a member of the EEC, is defined for this purpose as including England, Scotland, Wales, Northern Ireland and Gibraltar. The Channel Islands and the Isle of Man are not included;
- an employee in legal custody on the first day of incapacity.

An employee who thinks he has been wrongly denied SSP is entitled to:

(a) a written statement; and

(b) ask the adjudication officer in the local DHSS office for a decision.

Both employer and employee can appeal from the adjudication officer to a Social Security Appeal Tribunal, and from the Tribunal to a Social Security Commission. On a point of law, a further Appeal may be taken to the Court of Appeal or Court of Session in Scotland.

The employer decides how an employee is to notify illness. He may ask for a statement signed by the employee, but not for a medical certificate for the first 7 days of illness.

An employee in any member state of the EEC is entitled to SSP.

Rates

The amount of SSP depends on the employee's average earnings over the 8 weeks before the period of illness. At 6 April, 1986, the weekly rate was:

£46.75 when weekly earnings were over £74.50;
£39.20 for earnings between £55.50 and £74.50;
£36.60 for earnings over £38 and below £55.50.

There is no entitlement when average earnings are below the minimum for National Insurance contributions (£38).

SSP is payable at a daily rate, which is the weekly entitlement divided by the number of working days ('qualifying days') in the pay period. PAYE and National Insurance contributions must be deducted.

SSP is payable for 28 weeks of absence. Periods of illness separated by less than 8 weeks are added together until the total reaches 28 weeks. The employee must then apply for social security payments.

The employer reimburses himself for SSP by deducting the amount paid from remittances of National Insurance contributions made to the Collector of Taxes. He must keep records of payments made and recovered.

Employer's duties

The duties of an employer under SSP scheme are:

(a) to keep sickness records, including for each employee:

    (i)   dates of sickness lasting more than four days;

    (ii)   dates for which SSP was not paid and reasons;

    (iii)   the number of qualifying days in each period of incapacity;

(b) to keep records of SSP payments made;

(c) to give employees leaving the employment a 'Leaver's Certificate' (SSP1(L)) to pass on to the next employer if the employee has been absent for illness in the 8 weeks before leaving. Copies of all SSP(L)s must be kept for at least 3 years.

4   Financial management

Added value

As an economic concept, added value is not new, but its application to modern business is only a few years old. The concept is simple: added value is taken as being a company's sales revenue minus the cost of its materials and bought-in services. Wages costs are not included in the calculation: employees are regarded as receivers of part of the added value created, not part of the cost of producing it.

The logic of this is that while wages and salaries are in employees' pockets or banks, they are wealth and thus part of the added value created by their activities. Wages and salaries cease to be wealth when they are spent.

Measuring added value in this way is regarded as having a number of helpful uses.

- It is a useful indicator of productivity, which is a familiar word but which has no generally agreed definition. It is often taken as output related to certain factors of production, usually labour. However, it may also be thought of as being the relationship between input of capital, labour and raw materials and the output resulting from these resources. Added value, by applying a relatively simple and consistent measurement, makes it easier to compare productivity of companies. Since the concept can also be applied to various departments within a company it also offers comparisons between the productivity of various departments.
- Because added value can also be calculated on a per-employee basis and monitored from year to year, it offers a base on which annual pay awards can be negotiated. The level of a company's profits, on which many pay talks are based, provides no indication of productivity; in any case, the calculation of a company's profits is made at a particular time — the end of the company's financial year — and is likely to be out of date, as an indicator of performance, at the next round of pay talks.
- Regular monitoring of added value is a useful check on a company's continuing performance, with a decline in added value signalling possible problems ahead.
- Since added value can be measured against most items in a company's annual accounts, any problem areas are easy to identify.

Statements showing added value are already appearing in some companies' annual reports and accounts: the trend seems to be developing strongly. But there is no standard practice for accountants preparing added value statements and no standard definitions, for added value purposes, of the various items in the calculations required.

Meantime, added value, in its alternative form of value added, is, of course, already taxed as VAT. It is commonly seen as being the most cost-effective way of gathering tax so far devised.

Balance sheets

The balance sheet of a company is intended to show its overall financial position at the close of business on a particular date. It has two sections: one shows the assets and the other how those assets are financed.

Both sections of the balance sheet must add to the same total: the assets of a company cannot be financed by anything other than the money put into that business. Even when a company's assets (such as property) rise in value without any input of new money, the increase in the total assets value is matched by an increase in the 'reserves' item on the other side.

Company law requires companies to present the profit and loss account and balance sheet in standard formats. There are two standard formats for the balance sheet. Format 1 requires disclosure of 'net current assets'; format 2 does not. Once a company selects its format, it is expected to use it for subsequent years.

The choice of formats reflects the difficulty of achieving an absolute standardisation for all companies with their range of activities and sizes. A delivery van used by one company to distribute its products is a fixed asset. To a motor trader, a delivery van may be a current asset, expected to be sold and become cash within one year of balance sheet date.

The main headings on the 'assets employed' side of a balance sheet are: fixed assets (plant, machinery, buildings); current assets (stocks, debtors, investments, cash) and, perhaps surprisingly to anybody other than an accountant, current liabilities or creditors.

Current liabilities include bank overdrafts, tax due but not paid at balance sheet date and trade creditors (to whom money is owed at balance sheet date). The bank, the Inland Revenue and creditors are, in effect, helping to finance the company's business and the finance involved is short-term. The total of the assets side does not necessarily express a value on the basis of current day's value. It may be at book, or historical, value — the cost at the time of acquisition less any depreciation that the company and its auditors provide for.

Break-even point

Use of break-even techniques highlights the interplay of costs, prices and sales volume in a way which helps management to select the best of several possible courses of action. Calculation of break-even requires the accurate determination of both fixed and variable costs. Break-even is reached when total sales revenue equals both sets of costs.

By using a simple formula, managements can calculate the effect on profits of varying production volume or sales price. The first step is to work out the difference between sales revenue (actual or projected) and *variable* costs. This is called the *contribution* (towards the fixed costs).

Break-even is achieved when total contribution equals total fixed costs. This gives the general formula:

$$\text{Break-even (in units)} = \frac{\text{Total fixed costs}}{\text{Contribution per unit}}$$

The contribution is often expressed as a percentage of sales, called the contribution margin percentage or profit–volume ratio. The break-even point in sales value terms is arrived at by dividing fixed costs by the profit–volume ratio.

The formula makes it easy to calculate the effect on break-even point of varying the sales price per unit or of increasing or decreasing production. By using the technique regularly, as variables or market conditions change, management can take a view on appropriate courses of action.

To illustrate: take the case of a small garage which hires out a car at 40p per mile. In one accounting period the car is hired for 12,000 miles to give the following figures:

Revenue		£4,800
Costs		
Fixed	£2,400	
Variable	£1,920	
Total		£4,320
Profit		£480

The contribution (sales revenue minus variable costs) is £2,880: in unit terms (£2,800 divided by 12,000 miles) it is .24p.
Break-even (fixed costs divided by the contribution per unit) thus works out at 10,000 miles.
The profit–volume ratio (contribution as a percentage of sales — £2,880 as a percentage of £4,800 in the example) is 60 per cent.
Break-even in cash terms (fixed costs divided by the profit–volume ratio — £2,400 divided by .60) works out at £4,000.

Budgeting

Budgeting is a function of top management, but the process involves every line manager, department head and supervisor. An accepted principle of good budgeting is that everyone concerned with its construction and with achieving the targets set should be involved from the start.

Rolling budgets, in which the horizon of the budget is pushed forward each month, are now common. A company using this system is always a year ahead with its planning. It is usual, in rolling, and in some other forms of, budgeting, to project the first three months in detail, the next three months in less detail and the last six months in outline only.

For most companies, the budgeting process starts with a sales forecast broken down into volume, type and mix. Common practice is to express the forecast in units, rather than in cash revenue, at this stage.

Good practice requires that any sales forecast is made in close consultation with the marketing and promotion departments. Any sales forecast has to have behind it a properly thought-out marketing plan.

The aim of the sales forecast is to arrive at numbers which are reasonably capable of achievement, resisting a temptation to under-estimate, to be on the safe side.

Once settled, the sales forecasts need to be translated into production budgets to establish that the projections are within the company's productive capacity. Preparation of production budgets involves subsidiary budgets: work in progress; raw materials, labour, plant utilisation.

Assuming that the sales forecasts are within the company's capacity to produce, the production cost budget, that is normally the next stage in the overall budgeting process, is critical. For most companies, these budgets normally include some provision for the unforeseeable.

Side by side with the development of production budgets is the preparation of budgets for selling and marketing, transport, distribution, research and development and administration, which includes the costs of the finance department and general management. Budgeting for overheads, fixed and variable, completes the cycle. It is a particularly difficult area to budget for. Although fixed overheads normally present no problems, the variables do. They are peculiar to each company and each needs to find its own solution: there are no general rules.

When all the costs involved in the process of producing the company's products are assembled, two further processes follow. Decisions on pricing are needed and sales revenue figures put to the sales forecast figures originally expressed in units. These figures can then be expressed in cash flow budgets so that the finance director can take a view on the company's need for finance in the budget period.

Cash flows and discounted cash flows

Cash flow is commonly used to mean the profit derived from a trading operation (after deducting tax and dividend payments), but adding back the depreciation charge for the year for the production equipment involved. Depreciation is added back because, while it is not a payment of cash, it is a notional expense, spreading the cost of acquiring an asset over its estimated effective life. (*See* pages 115–116 for a simple cash flow forecast excluding depreciation.)

Profit is thus not the same as cash flow. To illustrate: a company buys plant costing £250,000 and decides to depreciate it at £50,000 a year over a five-year estimated life. Revenue from sales over the first full year of production amounts to £500,000 and total operating costs to £350,000. The actual net inflow of cash from the operation (profit) is £150,000 for the year. But, because the depreciation charge of £50,000 is added back, the cash flow for the same period is £200,000. If sales revenue and operating costs remain the same over the five-year period, the profit and the cash flow are the same for the whole life of the project. This is because the original outlay of £250,000 on the equipment is represented by the depreciation charge of £50,000 over the five years. Depreciation apart, there are other reasons why cash flows do not equate with profit. A new project rarely starts at the precise beginning of a company's accounting year; tax is not necessarily paid in the same accounting period; customers take time to pay.

These and related factors are important in compiling discounted cash flows, used to guide management in appraising projected investments of capital on a particular venture. Cash flows are discounted, for this purpose, because cash in hand now is worth more than the same amount due to be received at some future date. Cash in hand can now be invested: at an interest rate of 15 per cent, £1,000 becomes £1,150 after a year. After two years the original £1,000 accumulates to £1,322.50. Thus, £1,322.50 due to be received in two years' time is seen as being equivalent to £1,000 received now — usually called its net present value.

Discounted cash flows

The tables (*see* pages 117–121) show the present values of cash amounts which will be receivable or payable in future periods from 1 year to 20 years at interest rates of 1 per cent per annum to 30 per cent per annum.

They answer the questions: 'How much is a sum of money which I shall receive in the future worth today?' Or, 'How much must be invested today to accumulate to a given sum at the end of a number of years?' For example, a company has to make a payment of £58,000 at the end of a six-year period. What sum must it invest today to accumulate to £58,000 at the end of six years, if the rate of interest on invested funds is 9 per cent per annum?

Select the column headed 9 per cent and move down to year 6. The relevant factor is 0.5963. Multiply this by the amount required in the future to give:

$$0.5963 \times £58,000 = \textbf{£34,585}$$

The tables may also be used to evaluate investments when payments and receipts of cash are involved.

A company is invited to participate in a joint venture. It will be required to put up £150,000 immediately as its share of the venture capital. The estimated cash flows it will receive back are £30,000 at the end of year one, £35,000 at the end of year two, £45,000 at the end of year three, £55,000 at the end of year four and finally £65,000 at the end of year five. The company can borrow funds at 11 per cent per annum. Is it worthwhile participating in the joint venture? Each of the individual cash flows is valued at today's terms using the tables to give the following results:

Initial cash investment		Receipts	Payments
			150,000
End of year 1	0.9009 x £30,000 =	27,027	
End of year 2	0.8116 x £35,000 =	28,406	
End of year 3	0.7312 x £45,000 =	32,904	
End of year 4	0.6587 x £55,000 =	36,229	
End of year 5	0.5935 x £65,000 =	38,578	
	Totals	163,144	
		150,000	150,000
Net Present Value (NPV)		£13,144	

The investment in the joint venture is estimated to yield the sum of £13,144 after taking account of interest at 11 per cent. To put it another way, the net present value of the cash flows is £13,144.

A cash flow forecast—excluding depreciation

Item	Jan	Feb	Mar	Apr	May	Jun	Jul	Aug	Sep	Oct	Nov	Dec	Year
CASH INFLOWS													
Sales volume, units	2000	1700	1800	2100	2300	2400	2500	2200	2000	2000	1900	2000	24900
Unit price, £	1.5	1.5	1.5	1.7	1.7	1.7	2	2	2	2	2	2	1.81
Sales revenue, £	3000	2550	2700	3570	3910	4080	5000	4400	4000	4000	3800	4000	45010
Cash sales, £	300	255	270	357	391	408	500	440	400	400	380	400	4501
Credit sales, £	2700	2295	2430	3213	3519	3672	4500	3960	3600	3600	3420	3600	40509
Bad debts, £	54	46	49	64	70	73	90	79	72	72	68	72	809
Recoverable credit sales, £	2646	2249	2381	3149	3449	3599	4410	3881	3528	3528	3352	3528	39700
Credit length, months	1	1	1	1	1	1	1	1	1	1	1	1	
Cash from credit sales, £	2300	2646	2249	2381	3149	3449	3599	4410	3881	3528	3528	3352	38472
Total cash inflow, £	2600	2901	2519	2738	3540	3857	4099	4850	4281	3928	3908	3752	42973

Item	Jan	Feb	Mar	Apr	May	Jun	Jul	Aug	Sep	Oct	Nov	Dec	Year
CASH OUTFLOWS													
Cash paid to employees, £	684	684	821	821	821	1027	1027	1027	1027	1027	1027	1027	11020
NI and PAYE paid, £	418	418	418	501	501	501	626	626	626	626	626	626	6513
Material costs, £	1080	1260	1380	1440	1500	1320	1600	1600	1520	1600	1600	1440	17340
Rent, £	100	100	100	100	100	100	100	100	100	100	100	100	1200
Rates, £	50	50	50	50	50	50	50	50	50	50	50	50	600
Utilities, £	50	50	50	50	50	50	50	50	50	50	50	50	600
Other overheads, £	60	70	30	40	80	40	30	20	50	60	50	40	570
Total non-labour costs, £	1340	1530	1610	1680	1780	1560	1830	1820	1770	1860	1850	1680	20310
Credit taken, months	–	–	–	–	–	–	–	–	–	–	–	–	
Non-labour costs paid, £	1500	1340	1530	1610	1680	1780	1560	1830	1820	1770	1860	1850	20130
VAT paid/(received), £	148	0	0	570	0	0	932	0	0	1119	0	0	2769
Corporation tax paid, £	0	0	0	0	0	0	0	0	2500	0	0	0	2500
Interest paid, £	100	118	118	118	125	128	123	121	115	118	133	136	1453
Total cash outflow, £	2850	2560	2887	3620	3127	3436	4268	3604	6088	4660	3646	3639	44385
CASH BALANCES													
Opening balance, £	–10000	–10250	–9909	–10277	–11159	–10746	–10325	–10494	–9248	–11055	–11787	–11525	–10000
Cash inflows, £	2600	2901	2519	2738	3540	3857	4099	4850	4281	3928	3908	3752	42973
Cash outflows, £	2850	2560	2887	3620	3127	3436	4268	3604	6088	4660	3646	3639	44385
Closing balance, £	–10250	–9909	–10277	–11159	–10746	–10325	–10494	–9248	–11055	–11787	–11525	–11412	–11412

Discounted cash flows

			Percentage			
Year	1	2	3	4	5	6
1	0.9901	0.9804	0.9709	0.9615	0.9524	0.9434
2	0.9803	0.9612	0.9426	0.9246	0.9070	0.8900
3	0.9706	0.9423	0.9151	0.8890	0.8638	0.8396
4	0.9610	0.9238	0.8885	0.8548	0.8227	0.7921
5	0.9515	0.9057	0.8626	0.8219	0.7835	0.7473
6	0.9420	0.8880	0.8375	0.7903	0.7462	0.7050
7	0.9327	0.8706	0.8131	0.7599	0.7107	0.6651
8	0.9235	0.8535	0.7894	0.7307	0.6768	0.6274
9	0.9143	0.8368	0.7664	0.7026	0.6446	0.5919
10	0.9053	0.8203	0.7441	0.6756	0.6139	0.5584
11	0.8963	0.8043	0.7224	0.6496	0.5847	0.5268
12	0.8874	0.7885	0.7014	0.6246	0.5568	0.4970
13	0.8787	0.7730	0.6810	0.6006	0.5303	0.4688
14	0.8700	0.7579	0.6611	0.5775	0.5051	0.4423
15	0.8613	0.7430	0.6419	0.5553	0.4810	0.4173
16	0.8528	0.7284	0.6232	0.5339	0.4581	0.3936
17	0.8444	0.7142	0.6050	0.5134	0.4363	0.3714
18	0.8360	0.7002	0.5874	0.4936	0.4155	0.3503
19	0.8277	0.6864	0.5703	0.4746	0.3957	0.3305
20	0.8195	0.6730	0.5537	0.4564	0.3769	0.3118

Percentage

Year	7	8	9	10	11	12
1	0.9346	0.9259	0.9174	0.9091	0.9009	0.8929
2	0.8734	0.8573	0.8417	0.8264	0.8116	0.7972
3	0.8163	0.7938	0.7722	0.7513	0.7312	0.7118
4	0.7629	0.7350	0.7084	0.6830	0.6587	0.6355
5	0.7130	0.6806	0.6499	0.6209	0.5935	0.5674
6	0.6663	0.6302	0.5963	0.5645	0.5346	0.5066
7	0.6228	0.5835	0.5470	0.5132	0.4817	0.4523
8	0.5820	0.5403	0.5019	0.4665	0.4339	0.4039
9	0.5439	0.5002	0.4604	0.4241	0.3909	0.3606
10	0.5083	0.4632	0.4224	0.3855	0.3522	0.3220
11	0.4751	0.4289	0.3875	0.3505	0.3173	0.2875
12	0.4440	0.3971	0.3555	0.3186	0.2858	0.2567
13	0.4150	0.3677	0.3262	0.2897	0.2575	0.2292
14	0.3878	0.3405	0.2992	0.2633	0.2320	0.2046
15	0.3624	0.3152	0.2745	0.2394	0.2090	0.1827
16	0.3387	0.2919	0.2519	0.2176	0.1883	0.1631
17	0.3166	0.2703	0.2311	0.1978	0.1696	0.1456
18	0.2959	0.2502	0.2120	0.1799	0.1528	0.1300
19	0.2765	0.2317	0.1945	0.1635	0.1377	0.1161
20	0.2584	0.2145	0.1784	0.1486	0.1240	0.1037

Percentage

Year	13	14	15	16	17	18
1	0.8850	0.8772	0.8696	0.8621	0.8547	0.8475
2	0.7831	0.7695	0.7561	0.7432	0.7305	0.7182
3	0.6931	0.6750	0.6575	0.6407	0.6244	0.6086
4	0.6133	0.5921	0.5718	0.5523	0.5337	0.5158
5	0.5428	0.5194	0.4972	0.4761	0.4561	0.4371
6	0.4803	0.4556	0.4323	0.4104	0.3898	0.3704
7	0.4251	0.3996	0.3759	0.3538	0.3332	0.3139
8	0.3762	0.3506	0.3269	0.3050	0.2848	0.2660
9	0.3329	0.3075	0.2843	0.2630	0.2434	0.2255
10	0.2946	0.2697	0.2472	0.2267	0.2080	0.1911
11	0.2607	0.2366	0.2149	0.1954	0.1778	0.1619
12	0.2307	0.2076	0.1869	0.1685	0.1520	0.1372
13	0.2042	0.1821	0.1625	0.1452	0.1299	0.1163
14	0.1807	0.1597	0.1413	0.1252	0.1110	0.0985
15	0.1599	0.1401	0.1229	0.1079	0.0949	0.0835
16	0.1415	0.1229	0.1069	0.0930	0.0811	0.0708
17	0.1252	0.1078	0.0929	0.0802	0.0693	0.0600
18	0.1108	0.0946	0.0808	0.0691	0.0592	0.0508
19	0.0981	0.0829	0.0703	0.0596	0.0506	0.0431
20	0.0868	0.0728	0.0611	0.0514	0.0433	0.0365

Percentage

Year	19	20	21	22	23	24
1	0.8403	0.8333	0.8264	0.8197	0.8130	0.8065
2	0.7062	0.6944	0.6830	0.6719	0.6610	0.6504
3	0.5934	0.5787	0.5645	0.5507	0.5374	0.5245
4	0.4987	0.4823	0.4665	0.4514	0.4369	0.4230
5	0.4190	0.4019	0.3855	0.3700	0.3552	0.3411
6	0.3521	0.3349	0.3186	0.3033	0.2888	0.2751
7	0.2959	0.2791	0.2633	0.2486	0.2348	0.2218
8	0.2487	0.2326	0.2176	0.2038	0.1909	0.1789
9	0.2090	0.1938	0.1799	0.1670	0.1552	0.1443
10	0.1756	0.1615	0.1486	0.1369	0.1262	0.1164
11	0.1476	0.1346	0.1228	0.1122	0.1026	0.0938
12	0.1240	0.1122	0.1015	0.0920	0.0834	0.0757
13	0.1042	0.0935	0.0839	0.0754	0.0678	0.0610
14	0.0876	0.0779	0.0693	0.0618	0.0551	0.0492
15	0.0736	0.0649	0.0573	0.0507	0.0448	0.0397
16	0.0618	0.0541	0.0474	0.0415	0.0364	0.0320
17	0.0520	0.0451	0.0391	0.0340	0.0296	0.0258
18	0.0437	0.0376	0.0323	0.0279	0.0241	0.0208
19	0.0367	0.0313	0.0267	0.0229	0.0196	0.0168
20	0.0308	0.0261	0.0221	0.0187	0.0159	0.0135

Percentage

Year	25	26	27	28	29	30
1	0.8000	0.7937	0.7874	0.7813	0.7752	0.7692
2	0.6400	0.6299	0.6200	0.6104	0.6009	0.5917
3	0.5120	0.4999	0.4882	0.4768	0.4658	0.4552
4	0.4096	0.3968	0.3844	0.3725	0.3611	0.3501
5	0.3277	0.3149	0.3027	0.2910	0.2799	0.2693
6	0.2621	0.2499	0.2383	0.2274	0.2170	0.2072
7	0.2097	0.1983	0.1877	0.1776	0.1682	0.1594
8	0.1678	0.1574	0.1478	0.1388	0.1304	0.1226
9	0.1342	0.1249	0.1164	0.1084	0.1011	0.0943
10	0.1074	0.0992	0.0916	0.0847	0.0784	0.0725
11	0.0859	0.0787	0.0721	0.0662	0.0607	0.0558
12	0.0687	0.0625	0.0568	0.0517	0.0471	0.0429
13	0.0550	0.0496	0.0447	0.0404	0.0365	0.0330
14	0.0440	0.0393	0.0352	0.0316	0.0283	0.0254
15	0.0352	0.0312	0.0277	0.0247	0.0219	0.0195
16	0.0281	0.0248	0.0218	0.0193	0.0170	0.0150
17	0.0225	0.0197	0.0172	0.0150	0.0132	0.0116
18	0.0180	0.0156	0.0135	0.0118	0.0102	0.0089
19	0.0144	0.0124	0.0107	0.0092	0.0079	0.0068
20	0.0115	0.0098	0.0084	0.0072	0.0061	0.0053

Cash management

Cash management, in its modern, mainly electronic form, is based on increasingly sophisticated information processing techniques. It has grown out of the recognition that information, provided promptly and accurately, is as important as money itself.

In its basic form, cash management is the process of determining and maintaining the proper level of cash within a company. A cash manager's functions are to:

- speed the conversion of payments by the company's customers into usable bank deposits;
- control the outflow of payments;
- concentrate company funds into a central account where they can most easily be controlled;
- put cash surplus to requirement to work, by investment or acquisition.

His ability to perform these functions has been both helped and greatly enhanced by the development of electronic funds transfer (EFT), both nationally and internationally. Within EFT the introduction of techniques for carrying and distributing methods known as packet-switching systems (PSS) has both cheapened the costs of EFT and increased the efficiency of the system.

It does so by breaking down a body of information to be transmitted electronically from one centre to another into separate packages. Whereas in a telephone or telex call both parties are maintaining a constant transmission path, PSS interleaves packages of information from various sources, delivering them in the right order at the destination. The best known application of PSS to the banking system is the international banking network SWIFT (Society for Worldwide Interbank Financial Telecommunications). It is a method of conveying instructions to transfer money — not in itself a method of transferring funds. Well over 1,000 banks from 50 or more countries use the system which handles over half a million transactions a day.

In the United Kingdom, the clearing banks have introduced a new, electronic banking system for sending guaranteed, unconditional, sterling payments for same-day settlement from one bank, on behalf of itself or its customers, to another bank. The system is called CHAPS (Clearing House Automated Payments System). Regular payments made by bank customers under standing order arrangements are processed through another system — BACS (Bankers Automated Clearing System).

In step with these and other developments in the electronic funds transfer field is the equally rapid growth of electronic data providing services. The best known of these services is probably Reuters, which began life, in the 19th century, by using carrier pigeons to speed the transmission of foreign news to Britain, and which is now one of the major success stories of the mid-1980s.

As a consequence of these developments, a cash manager now has available both a constant stream of up-to-the-minute financial information of all kinds, national and international, and the means of putting his decisions into action immediately.

For many companies, cash management has moved from a subsidiary activity to one capable of contributing substantially to profits. Increasingly, the term 'treasury management' is replacing 'cash management'. The process is expected to continue as smaller firms automate their cash systems and begin to use the electronic transfer and information systems now on offer, and as the banks and information providers increase and improve still further their services to their customers.

Cost accounting

Cost accounting is concerned with determining the true costs of operations, processes, departments or products within a company: it is distinct from financial accounting, which is concerned with reporting on a company's finances to shareholders and others outside the company.

In theory, the cost of a product or service is merely the expenditure needed to produce it. In practice, even a small company producing a range of products may find it difficult to determine an accurate figure for the cost of producing one of those products. A cost accountant approaches the problem by classifying cost in various ways:

- direct or indirect;
- its nature — labour, materials;
- its function — production, marketing, distribution;
- its controllability;
- expected or unexpected;
- liability to change relative to changes in output volume;
- its relevance to the product.

Thereafter, the cost accounting framework is based on four distinct elements: uniform costing; absorption costing; marginal costing and variance accounting.

Uniform costing

The need for uniform costing arises in a group of companies where each company may have different costing techniques and practices. It is not a separate costing technique, merely the adoption by all concerned of common principles and practices. The main areas requiring uniform costing in a group of companies are:

- cost accounting periods;
- classification of accounts;
- treatment of overheads;
- cost centres;
- stock valuation;
- accounting principles;
- financial statements.

Absorption costing

Absorption costing is based on the theory that all costs incurred by a business should be charged to production. In practice, absorption costing systems do not always charge all costs and expenses to products or processes. It then becomes a principle whereby fixed as well as variable costs are allocated and apportioned to cost units; overheads are absorbed according to activity level where such overheads may be either total and relate to all functions, be production-based, or based upon some functional combination.

Marginal costing

Marginal costing avoids the problem of how to charge the overheads fairly and accurately to production.

All costs are classified as either fixed or variable and only the variable costs are charged to output. This means that profit per unit cannot be calculated because the total cost per unit will not be known. Instead of the unit profit calculated under absorption costing, a marginal costing system will produce a contribution per unit. The contribution each unit makes towards the fixed costs is often used as a key figure for price/output decisions. Two main features of a pure marginal costing system are the segregation of all costs into fixed and variable elements and the exclusion of all fixed costs from unit cost calculations.

Variance accounting

Variance accounting is a technique whereby the planned activities of an undertaking are quantified in budgets, standard costs, standard selling prices and standard profit margins, and the difference between these and the actual results are compared.

Current cost accounting

Companies preparing their annual financial statements can choose between applying two separate sets of accounting rules: historical cost accounting and current cost accounting.

The former requires the reporting company to value its assets at the cost incurred, at the time, of acquiring them; the latter allows the company to value them at their latest valuation or at current cost. Investments classed as fixed assets may be included at either their latest valuation or at a value determined on any basis that the directors of the company think appropriate.

A requirement of the relevant Companies Act is that a company using current cost accounting must state the basis of valuation of each item affected and, in each case, give either the historical cost amounts or the difference between these amounts and the current cost amounts.

Current cost accounting is intended to bring into account the effect of inflation in measuring the value of a company's assets. It has many advocates as a means of producing an accurate picture of a company's financial position. But it is not generally accepted by a majority of companies. The common view appears to be that both historical cost accounting and current cost accounting procedures should be used by the larger companies.

The choice between the two sets of accounting rules is a significant one for a company. Accounts prepared under current cost accounting rules usually show a smaller profit than those based on historical cost accounting. This is because of the basic fact in company life: when a company is formed, money raised from shareholders is invested in productive business assets. Historical cost accounting maintains the money value of the shareholders' original investment by charging against the company's income the cost of resources, at original value, used in trading activity. Current cost profit is the balance left after full provision for the replacement cost of assets used. Current cost accounting thus is concerned with maintaining a company's capacity to produce.

The difference between current cost profit and historical cost profit varies considerably between various sectors. In general, the faster the rate of growth in costs, the greater the difference. But in no case is the difference insignificant.

The fact that current cost accounting produces lower profit figures is regarded as one of its attractions, since the reporting company's tax liability is correspondingly reduced. A further consideration is that lower profits strengthen managements' hands in seeking to reduce wage claims in collective bargaining processes.

It appears to be widely accepted that there is a strong case for companies to adopt current cost accounting, for a variety of reasons; underlying them all is the belief that it is a more accurate way of measuring performance during a period of inflation. The fact that it has not been more widely accepted reflects the view that historical cost data is readily available, broadly factual (there is no scope of subjective value judgments), easily verified and well understood.

Depreciation

The acquisition of a substantial asset by a company involves the expenditure of capital. By depreciating the original cost of the asset over a period, the company makes provision for the recovery of that cost by the end of the asset's productive life.

Essential Facts for Managers

For most public companies, provision of depreciation for assets is a legal requirement: a public company must not pay dividends out of capital.

In general, depreciation is calculated for four practical purposes:

(a) to calculate liability to tax: the Inland Revenue have their own rules for the calculation of depreciation based broadly on current business practice;

(b) valuation of the asset for purchase or sale second-hand;

(c) to calculate with reasonable accuracy, making due allowance for the cost of acquiring the asset, the net profit arising from the asset's use;

(d) to help calculate a proper pricing policy for the product or service created by the asset.

There is no generally agreed, single method of providing for depreciation in a company's accounts. Some of those used are set out below.

Fixed instalment

The cost of the asset is reduced by equal annual instalments over a fixed number of years. The amount depreciated each year is calculated simply by dividing the cost of the asset by the number of years of its estimated effective life.

Reducing balance

A fixed percentage is written off the diminishing value of the asset each year. This method provides relatively high depreciation charges in the first year or two of the asset's life, when repairs and maintenance costs are likely to be light.

Revaluation

The difference between the original cost and the valuation placed on the asset at the end of the financial period. The method is used mostly for relatively low-value assets such as small tools.

Annuity system

The capital expended on acquiring the asset is regarded as earning a fixed rate of interest and depreciation is calculated on the base of interest foregone. The calculation is fairly complicated and, in general, the method is not widely used. It is regarded as being most appropriate for depreciating the value of a lease over a long period.

Sinking fund

An amount of cash equal to the depreciation each year is invested and allowed to accumulate at compound interest, in order to achieve sufficient capital to replace the asset at a fixed date in the future. The method has the advantage of providing actual cash for asset replacement, as distinct from other methods which make no such provision.

Insurance

Instead of investing in securities, a company purchases an endowment policy timed to mature when replacement will become due.

Factoring

As a generality, one fifth of a company's annual turnover is likely to be outstanding in the form of trade debts. The function of a factor is to buy these debts from the company and provide three services: the immediate payment of the sum agreed for the purchase of the debts; underwriting the credit risk; administration of the sales ledger of the client company.

Factoring is not suitable for all companies at all times. Trade credit is usually a proportionately larger item in the accounts of small and medium companies than in the larger ones, particularly in the early years. For such companies the relatively high fees charged by a factor (high compared with the costs of other forms of obtaining finance) can be set off against improved cash flow, efficient management of its sales ledger, staff-saving, saving in management time and lower overheads.

Factoring is not likely to help a company in decline, with shrinking turnover and poor growth potential. The cost to the company of the factor's services will become an increasingly substantial proportion of a falling turnover; for the factor, the returns will become increasingly less remunerative.

For a growing, young and well-managed company, however, factoring may well have benefits, and factors generally prefer such companies as their clients.

FIFO and LIFO

The valuation of stock and of work-in-progress at the end of a company's financial year is, for most businesses, an imprecise calculation. Human error can account for part of the imprecision, but its main source is the difficulty of placing a value on the total quantity of stock held, however subject to error that quantity may be.

In a company's annual report and accounts, stocks are usually presented at either the cost of buying them or, if lower, at net realisable value. However, stock is acquired over a period and at different, usually increasing, prices: not all the unsold stock at the end of the financial year will have been bought at the same price.

The 'First In, First Out' (FIFO) method assumes that the items first received are those first sold and that stock remaining was acquired at the latest, highest, prices. 'Last In, First Out' (LIFO) assumes each sale is from the last lot received: when sales exceed the amount of this last lot, they are taken as coming from the previous batch. Stock is valued at the lowest prices paid. Stock valuation is thus higher under the FIFO method than under LIFO: consequently FIFO produces a higher profit figure in the report and accounts.

It is claimed for FIFO that it produces a more accurate picture of the true position; LIFO, it is claimed, works better during a period of inflation.

The Financial Services Act 1986

The Financial Services Act makes it a criminal offence for any person(s) to engage in investment business without first obtaining authorisation.

Investments covered by the Act include: shares, debentures, government and public securities, warrants, certificates representing securities, unit trusts, options, futures, contracts for differences, long-term insurance contracts and rights and interests in any of these investments.

The Act does *not* include bank accounts, property, works of art, stamps, coins, and precious metals (unless they are subject to contract for future delivery).

A person is regarded as carrying on an investment business if he:

- deals in investments;
- arranges deals in investments;
- manages investments;
- advises on investments,
- acts in connection with a collective investment scheme (unit trusts).

The Act provides for a limited range of exemptions: they include underwriting agents at Lloyds, recognised investment exchanges and money market institutions as listed by the Bank of England.

Supervisory powers for the regulation of investment business is delegated to the Securities and Investments Board (SIB) at 3, Royal Exchange Buildings, London EC3V 3NL (tel: 01-283 2474).

In turn, the SIB will rely on Self-Regulating Organisations (SROs) to control particular aspects of the financial services industry. Although a number of bodies were expected, at the time of printing, to apply for recognition as SROs, formal recognition and the precise definitions of their scope will not be finalised until well into 1987.

The impact of the Act is considerable and covers a number of firms who would not normally regard themselves as being in the investment business. Such firms might include: insurance brokers who advise on or sell life assurance; estate agents and surveyors who arrange endowment mortgages; pension fund trustees who take part in the day-to-day management of a scheme's investments, company treasurers who advise on investments of companies which are not part of their group.

Fixed and variable costs

It is often said that all costs are variable in the long run, if only because inflation will constantly push up prices and wage costs. However, in practice, in cost accounting a particular business operation, distinctions need to be made between fixed, variable and semi-variable costs. Fixed costs are those which remain the same at all levels of activity. Thus, unit costs for fixed expenses vary inversely with the volume of output. In the short term, these are relatively easy to identify: they include rent of premises, insurance, management salaries and local rates.

Variable costs are those which vary with changes in the level of activity: they include raw materials, labour costs and higher power consumption.

Semi-variable costs, which include the cost of employing casual labour, outworkers, repairs and general maintenance, vary with the volume of output, but less strongly than variable costs.

Foreign exchange management

Any company having to pay or receive money in a currency other than its local currency is exposed to the risk of unfavourable fluctuations in the exchange rate between the two currencies. The risk varies with the currency concerned, the amount involved and the duration of the exposure. A company involved in negotiating a large capital project and quoting in a foreign currency may have to allow for several years to elapse between first negotiations (and quotations) and receiving payment. At the other end of the scale an intending tourist may find his traveller's cheques a little cheaper if he buys them at a suitable moment.

A company facing a foreign exchange risk can hedge against that risk by creating another risk which is of the same amount, currency and timing as the original risk but in the opposite direction. It may not always be possible, because of exchange control or other restrictions, to create a perfectly identical (but opposite) hedge, but a partial hedge may be better than none.

A company treasurer seeking a hedge has several instruments available to him.

Forward foreign exchange contracts

Foreign exchange contracts, almost invariably with a bank, are either spot or forward. Because spot contracts normally put a delivery date for the foreign exchange two business days ahead of agreement, they are not usually suitable as a hedging instrument. Forward contracts, however, are very suitable since they can be written for most currencies, in most amounts, for delivery at most future dates.

Forward foreign exchange options

There are two forms:

- The traditional option, in which a bank enters into a forward contract with a company, entitling the company to deliver the forward contract during a specified period in the future, but with the exchange rate under the contract predetermined, and the requirement to deliver the currency at some date within the option period.

    The principal disadvantage of this form of option is that the exchange rate will typically be at best (from the company's point of view) the poorest available during the delivery period.

    In fact, the rate will frequently be poorer even than that, particularly if the interest rate differential between the currencies is low, since the bank will wish to build an extra premium into the rate to reward itself for giving the option.

- The newer delivery option, where the fundamental option is to deliver or not (i.e. complete the contract).

This form of option gives the holder the right, but not the commitment, to buy (or sell) a specified amount of currency at an agreed rate on the payment of a fee to the party which grants the option.

There are two styles of delivery option: (a) an American style option where the option may be exercised within a specified period; and (b) a European style where the option may be exercised only on a specified date.

Financial futures

There are now a number of relatively new open markets for forward currency contracts, known as futures markets. The principal futures markets are the London International Financial Futures Exchange (LIFFE) and the Chicago Mercantile Exchange. These contracts may be regarded as an adjunct to forward contracts available from banks and generally have the following advantages and disadvantages, compared with such bank-generated forward contracts:

- the rates obtainable in the futures market are generally very fine;

- very large transactions can often be effected without moving the market as a whole;
- however, the amounts of the contracts and the value dates are both predetermined and inflexible, and the number of currencies available is still very limited.

Accordingly, these markets will usually only be suitable for those with a very large volume of transactions, and in conjunction with other hedging techniques.

Swaps

A swap is an agreement to purchase/sell one currency for a second, for one value date (usually spot) and sell/purchase the first currency for the second for a different value date. The exchange rate used for the two value dates is usually the same and one of the parties will make a payment or series of semi-annual or annual payments reflecting the cost of the swap.

Swaps are generally available for longer periods than forward foreign exchange contracts and the counterparty may either be a bank or another company.

Swaps are commonly used to provide hedges on foreign currency loans or investments with a limited life. In the case of a loan, the currency proceeds are sold spot for local currency at drawdown, and a forward repurchase contract taken out as the second arm of the swap. The operation can be repeated as often as wanted, and the cost of the loan then becomes the foreign currency interest rate plus the cost (or less the benefit) of the swap. Under certain circumstances, this may result in cheaper borrowing than straight local currency.

A hedge for an asset representing a long position works in reverse. Local currency is sold spot to make the investment, and repurchased forward.

Forfaiting

Forfaiting is a financing tool used by exporters of capital and semi-capital goods of high value whose buyers want to spread payments over several years.

The financial institution providing the facilities purchases the exporting company's receivables — the payment due for the goods exported — for cash and, for a consideration, undertakes the commercial risk of the importer paying over an agreed period. The costs to the exporter of forfaiting vary from deal to deal. The forfaiting institution will charge the cost of funding the transaction and add a margin which may range between 0.5 per cent (for good risks) to eight per cent (for high risks).

London is now the most important centre of the forfait market.

Franchising

Franchising is an arrangement between a franchisor who, having successfully developed a product or service, passes to a franchisee the right to exploit that product or service in a particular area.

It is a very well established business practice in the United States where the franchised sales of goods and services are currently around 250 billion dollars, from almost 500,000 outlets. Strong growth is predicted both in the United States and in Britain. Franchising agreements differ, but they usually provide for the franchisor to undertake national or local advertising and general sales promotion, provide training for the franchisee and his staff, help with financing the franchisee, provide administrative support and take an active role in setting up the franchise. The franchisee usually pays the franchisor royalties on sales and a sum for setting-up costs. But he owns the equipment involved, buys his own stock, owns or rents the premises and retains the goodwill.

For the franchisor, franchising can yield a number of benefits: increased market penetration; expanding sales; dedicated branch managers; corporate growth with limited capital investment. The franchisee will benefit from bulk-buying discounts; help, financial and other, in setting up and running the business; the know-how and support of the franchisor.

Nevertheless, many franchise arrangements are not successful. This is sometimes because the franchisor has not properly planned his overall franchising operation; or because he has not chosen the right franchisee. For the franchisee, the control to which he has to submit can prove irksome: the need to pay royalties on sales will reduce profits, although not necessarily profitability. It is not unknown for a particular franchise to end simply because the franchisee was *too* successful.

Gearing

The capital structure of a company — the means by which it finances the acquisition of its assets — usually has two basic elements. Some of the capital is in the form of loans on which the company pays a pre-determined rate of interest; the remainder comes from the money paid by shareholders for their shares.

The relationship between loan and shareholder capital — the company's capital 'gearing' — is an important factor both for the company itself and for its potential investors.

The loan element in the capital structure may be in the form of debentures, bank overdraft and other forms of long-term borrowing. But it all has two important characteristics: it attracts the regular payment of interest, irrespective of the company's fortunes, and this interest has to be paid before the shareholders can get a dividend.

Together with preference shares, which give holders a fixed rate of dividend (not interest), these items in a company's balance sheet are known as its prior capital. Calculation of a company's gearing ratio is a simple division:

$$\frac{\text{Preference shares} + \text{long-term debt}}{\text{Ordinary shares}} \times 100$$

In general, for a low-geared company the figure would come out at around 50 per cent; 100 indicates a medium gearing and 150 a high gearing.

Prior capital is usually cheaper than shareholder capital and can be an attractive source of finance. But companies with a high gearing have a relatively high level of interest payments to make. This affects profits after tax, in which the ordinary shareholders are interested. For an expanding company, using prior capital to finance assets for further development in a favourable climate, a high gearing can be beneficial to all concerned. In less favourable conditions, high gearing, with its prior requirement to meet interest charges, can depress profits.

Inflation

Inflation, usually defined as a persistent rise in general price levels, can be one of two main types: cost-push or demand-pull. The first results from increases in the costs of key inputs; the second from an excess of demand over supply.

In practice, the distinction is not always easy to draw. The position is blurred, in any case, by the inflationary expectations that a persistent rise in prices always generates. Companies who build in expected price rises into their costings; unions who seek wage rises to 'beat' inflation; consumers who increase or accelerate their purchases for the same reason — all contribute to prolonging inflation and, mostly, to pushing the rate of inflation higher. Inflation is commonly thought of as relating to a period in which price rises are both general and noticeable. A degree of inflation, however, is regarded as inevitable and only very rarely, and then only for short periods, has the rate of inflation fallen to zero or to a negative figure. The last such occasion was during the depression of the 1930s.

Although there is no consensus on the point, an inflation rate of 1–2 per cent would be regarded as both normal and acceptable by many economists. Government intervention, when the rate starts to move above these levels, can slow or, sometimes, stop further increases in the rate. If, however, the rate continues to rise and the country as a whole begins to build inflationary expectations into their calculations, the process is hard to stop. It is only when inflationary expectations start to ease off that the end of a period of high inflation may be in sight.

Insurance

Government regulations concerning insurance are administered by the Department of Trade (Insurance Division) which classifies all types of insurance business as set out below.

Property (exc. Motor)

- Fire and special perils
- Burglary and theft
- Machinery breakdown
- Cash-in-safe
- Cash-in-transit

Pecuniary

- Consequential loss following fire and perils
- Consequential loss following machinery breakdown
- Fidelity guarantee
- Credit
- Legal expenses
- Bonds

Legal liability

- Employees
- Public
  - (i) General (inc. boilers and lifts)
  - (ii) Products
- Professional

Personal accident

- For all staff
- For selected staff
  - (i) Directors and key personnel
  - (ii) Commercial travellers
  - (iii) Employees taking money to bank
  - (iv) On overseas assignments

Medical expenses

- On lines of 'Personal accident'

Motor

- Vehicles owned by insured
- Insured's liability for staff-owned cars used on business

There is no fixed tariff scale of rating for any of the classes in the following list. Premiums are graded according to the claims history, hazards and exposures of individual risks.

Property

(a) Fire and other perils

Rates for each peril are usually small relative to the fire rate. An overall figure is used according to the extras selected from — aircraft, riot, explosion, malicious damage, impact from vehicles, sprinkler leakage, storm and tempest, flood (excluding subsidence, heave and landslip).

The fire rate takes into account any sprinkler installation as well as fire extinguishing apparatus. Discounts are allowed for a 'deductible' (analogous to an excess on a motor policy) and also for agreement to continue the insurance for a number of years.

If a property is totally destroyed by fire and the owner has failed to insure for its full value, he will be the loser. But if there is only partial damage (which can be rectified by repair), then the insurer is penalised because he has not received the full premium. Partly for this reason, but more especially because of inflation, commercial risk policies are subject to the 'average' clause. The effect in the foregoing example would be that the insurer would be liable only for that portion of the repair cost which the sum insured would bear to the full value. This is known as 'full value' average but there are some types which only apply the principle if the sum insured is, for example, less than 75% of the full value.

The premium is developed by applying the rate to the sum insured which, ideally, should represent the value at the time of loss. Fire rates on contents are usually higher than those for buildings, and rating differentials can cause problems with 'floating' policies, which apply a single sum insured to a number of locations.

Stock

There are three classes of stock for insurance purposes: purchases, work-in-progress and finished goods. Purchases are insured at cost plus any delivery charges not included. Completed stock value will include direct costs (such as factory wages). Work-in-progress is valued mid-way between. Overhead costs are usually the subject of a consequential loss policy.

Because of daily variations in each of the three stock values, it is usual to have a 'Declaration' policy. A maximum figure (unlikely to be reached) is agreed at renewal for the ensuing year and a provisional premium of 75% paid, applying these figures to the relative rate. At the end of each month (or quarter) the insured submits a 'stock declaration' to the company and these are averaged at the end of the year — to produce an additional or refund premium. Full cover is thus equitably maintained.

Other contents

The most important item will be machinery and plant. It is usual to summarise (e.g. fixtures and fittings should be mentioned) and finish with 'and all other contents'. However, it may be necessary to isolate machinery and plant for insurance on a 'reinstatement value' basis. Such a policy guarantees 'new for old' (without depreciation allowance), providing the sum insured comprises new replacement costs and that, if there is a claim, physical replacement occurs.

Buildings

Determination of sums insured on buildings presents problems. At one end of the scale, a recently constructed property can be insured on a replacement basis (i.e. contract price loaded for inflation). What about a dilapidated old building which occupies a valuable site? The expressions 'market value' and 'book value' usually have to be qualified and the best approach is: 'What would we do after a serious fire?'

All risks

This type of cover is normally associated with works of art, trophies and so on, but competition has caused some insurers to extend the conventional 'fire and perils' wording to include accidental loss and damage. Naturally, rates are higher. Wordings differ and to some extent the expression 'all risks' is a misnomer because, inevitably, there will be policy exclusions.

'Contractors' all risks' policies include damage to construction work in progress and liability to employees and the public.

Theft (excluding cash)

The Theft Act ended the old distinction between burglary (forcible entry) and larceny (theft in the old sense). Commercial risks are usually restricted to theft following forcible entry because of the prevalence of shop-lifting and dishonesty of employees. A Lloyds' 'Jewellers' block policy' is an exception to this generality.

Cash

It is obligatory for large amounts of cash to be kept in a locked safe when the premises are closed and sometimes even during business hours, although a 'hold-up' can be insured. A maximum limit is fixed under each heading and a rate per cent applied.

Different arrangements apply to the insurance of cash-in-transit. Cash drawn from the bank for payment of wages is covered during the journey and on the premises until paid out. The premium is usually on a declaration basis, whereby an estimate of total annual carryings is furnished and a provisional premium paid against it. At the end of the year, the total of carryings is declared and an adjustment made. For the protection of the company there is usually a limit on any one carrying, which may or may not attract a separate premium.

Goods-in-transit

Cover can either be on a wide all-risks basis (with exclusions and a deductible), or for fire, collision and overturning (excluding theft, etc) which is cheaper.

Pecuniary loss

(a) Consequential loss

This is sometimes designated 'loss of profits' or 'business interruption' insurance. It indemnifies an insured for financial loss after physical destruction of property, and the nature of the policy is usually such that accounting advice is required. It is usual to cover, as a separate item, accountancy fees after a loss, on the lines of fees for architects after a physical loss.

Because of unknown trends and inflation, it is usual to insure on the same lines as a stock declaration policy; a top estimate is made in advance (and at every renewal) and a provisional premium paid at 75 per cent of this figure — with subsequent adjustment when the final figure is known.

The rate to be applied is the average contents rate of all premises insured and is obtained by adding up sums insured on contents (excluding buildings) and dividing it into the total contents premium.

Legal liability

(a) Employers

Premiums are based on the total wage roll, although where a degree of hazard exists between occupations, a differential is applied.

The system of estimating and adjustment applies. It is compulsory for an employer to insure and to display an appropriate certificate to his staff. The indemnity is £2 million under the Employers (Compulsory Insurance) Act 1969, but policies usually provide unlimited indemnity.

(b) Public

Employers can insure risks to the public in various ways because of the vicarious liability for actions of employees, and also as property owners. Liability for accidents in relation to lifts and pressure vessels is normally separately insured.

The rate of premium is applied to the overall wage roll, but will vary not only with hazard but with the selected limit of indemnity. Other methods of rating may be based on the number of employees, turnover or capacity (e.g. theatres and hotels). Small risks carry a flat premium.

(c) Products liability

An extension of the normal public liability cover is usually required by manufacturers, although retailers are sometimes technically liable. The difference between the ordinary cover and products is that, in the former case, injury or damage must be occasioned by an employee and in the latter, by the product itself. There is a need to limit liability for any one cause because there may be several simultaneous claims and an overall limit per year is usually also applied.

(d) Products guarantee

This is not insurable, but the cost of recalling defective goods producing a claim under (c) can be insured. Arrangements must be made in advance.

(e) Professional indemnity

Premiums are related to gross fees and the limit of indemnity required: in some professions' claims history has been so bad that only modest limits can be provided. Premiums used to be based on number of partners (at one rate) and staff (at another), but it is delegation which has produced the claims. Under the Companies Act 1981, directors and officers can be held liable in negligence and can be indemnified by separate insurance.

Personal accident

(a) For all staff

Premiums are directly related to the benefits — either for capital sums (for permanent disablement and death) — or to earnings. Capital sums will probably be expressed as a proportion of earnings, with perhaps a multiple for death or serious injury. If there is a 24 hour cover, the occupational risk will be taken into consideration.

Personal accident cover can be restricted to key personnel — directors, commercial travellers and those on trips abroad. All of these can either be on an annual adjustable or *ad hoc* basis.

Medical expenses

The object of a medical scheme is to provide families of employees with special protection; medical expenses are not covered under a personal accident policy unless special arrangements are made.

Motor

Premiums are graded according to the type of cover, which progresses from Act-only cover liability for third party and passenger injuries, through full third party only, third party fire and theft to comprehensive (probably subject to an excess). Care must be exercised to provide catastrophe cover if many vehicles (insured on limited terms) are garaged in one location. An employer must also insure the company's liability when employees are authorised to use their cars on company business; this may deprive them of the benefit of personal rating assessment.

Leasing

Leasing is now the largest single type of external finance for the acquisition of plant and equipment.

Growth in leasing arrangements as a means of acquiring equipment stems from changes in tax legislation, making such financing of interest to both lessor and lessee.

However, in March 1984 the Chancellor of the Exchequer announced radical changes to simplify the UK corporate tax scene. A significant single change was a realignment of the corporate tax burden by reducing considerably the tax benefits of acquiring equipment and, at the same time, reducing the rate at which tax is paid.

The Chancellor proposed a three-year transitional period; after 1986 the revised taxation structure reduces the potential benefits of leasing. These changes will have a significant effect on the leasing industry.

A lease is a contract between a lessor and a lessee for the hire of a specific asset. The lessor retains ownership of the asset, but conveys the right to the use of the asset to the lessee for an agreed period in return for the payment of specified rentals.

Essential Facts for Managers

The essential difference between a lease contract and a hire-purchase contract is that under a hire-purchase contract it is anticipated that ownership of the assets will pass to the lessee at some future date. This distinction is crucial from a tax standpoint. Under a lease, there is no such provision for title to pass to the lessee and, in theory, at the end of the term of the lease, the lessor has the right to use or dispose of the asset as he pleases.

Leases are generally of two types: finance leases and operating leases.

Finance leases

Finance leases are a method by which finance is provided to the lessee by the lessor. The lease terms are such that the lessor can expect to recover all, or substantially all, of his original investment from the contractual rental payments provided for in the lease. Thus, in general, the lessor assumes no commercial risks associated with the operating of the equipment, but his risks are essentially credit risks associated with the financial standing of the lessee, and to a certain extent the security given by the underlying value of the asset concerned. Similarly, the lessor expects none of the rewards of ownership of the asset, such as its eventual value.

Operating leases

In operating leases the lessor retains a substantial part of the risks and rewards of ownership. Thus, operating leases are for periods considerably shorter than the economic life of the asset, and the lessor will normally be responsible for insurance and maintenance of the asset. Unlike a finance lease, the lessee is not able accurately to assess the likely financial return from his investment at the outset. This will be dependent on such factors as:

- the eventual residual value compared to his original forecast;
- the actual economic life of the asset;
- insurance and maintenance costs during the life of the asset;
- the extent to which the equipment is hired out;
- the effects of inflation on rental income and operating costs.

In view of the significantly higher risks being undertaken by the lessor, he would normally expect a much higher return on his investment compared to that under a finance lease.

Life cycle costing

Life cycle costing takes into account both the initial capital cost of acquiring and installing an asset and the subsequent operating and maintenance costs over its estimated life.

The method requires predictions to be made before the acquisition decision; these predictions are subsequently modified, in the light of experience, over the asset's lifetime.

The following table, applying life cycle costing to the purchase of a copier, illustrates the method.

Life cycle costing

		Copier 'A'		Copier 'B'
Acquisition cost		£5,000		£4,000
Annual costs				
Maintenance	£500		£650	
Paper	£2,500		£3,500	
Operator's salary (part)	£3,500		£3,500	
Total	£6,500		£7,650	
Annual costs over est. 5 year life		£32,500		£38,250
Life cycle cost		£37,500		£42,250

The table takes account of higher maintenance agreement costs for the cheaper machine and the need to use more expensive, specialised paper.

Monetarism

There are two approaches to studying and influencing the country's economic performance: Keynesian and monetarist. The Keynesian approach concentrates on personal consumption which, it assumes, rises as incomes rise, although not by the same proportion. A government feeling the need to intervene to stabilise the economy can do so by changes in taxation levels and by injecting or withdrawing money — reflation and deflation.

Monetarism concentrates on the volume of money in the economy and the speed with which it circulates. It assumes that the speed of circulation is, relatively, constant so that consumption can be controlled by regulating the amount of money in circulation. Both approaches are generally regarded as intellectually respectable and both have their adherents.

Critics of monetarism argue that stability and growth in the economy, while welcome, may still leave the unemployment level unacceptably high. By injecting money into the economy in the form of public works, more jobs would be created: an increase in the rate of inflation which such action might precipitate would be preferable to higher unemployment levels.

Both approaches to economic policy may be coming under the influence of an increasingly significant development: the growth and size of the black economy. By its nature, the size of the black economy cannot be known with any accuracy, but it is generally accepted to be very large. Within the black economy money circulates faster than in the economy as a whole. Given the assumed size, this factor acts to counter the effects of a controlled money supply. If, as is thought possible, it fuels excessive growth in money supply, interest rates have to remain high to curb unacceptably high bank borrowings.

Profit margins

A company's gross profit margin is calculated by expressing the gross profit as a percentage of sales and, in stable business conditions, is likely to remain constant despite increases in turnover.

Gross profit is the excess of the selling price over the cost price and any direct costs involved in acquiring the goods sold. If, over a period, the gross profit margin falls significantly, several things may be happening to the company. The decline may simply reflect a decision to cut selling prices in order to remain competitive; the company may have had to pay more for its products and materials but, because of market conditions, has not been able to increase its selling prices proportionately; a change in the product mix may have caused variations in the overall profit margin, assuming individual lines earn differing gross profit percentages.

A further possibility, as shown up in the company's annual report and accounts, may be under- or over-valuation of stocks, since valuation of stock at the end of the financial year and the way it is calculated affects the profit shown in the accounts.

The net profit of a business takes into account its general overheads and a net profit percentage (net profit expressed as a percentage of sales) focuses attention on the profitability of business operations.

It is thus one method, among others, of measuring management success in conducting a business. More commonly, it is used to evaluate between different products in a product-mix operation.

5   Company law

Company law has been consolidated into four Acts which came into force on July 1, 1985. The Acts are:

The Companies Act 1985
The Business Names Act 1985
Company Securities (Insider Dealing) Act 1985
Companies Consolidation (Consequential
Provisions) Act 1985

The law has not been changed by these Acts, only re-arranged. It is administered by the Department of Trade and Industry.

Auditing

All limited companies, private and public, are required by law to appoint an independent auditor to examine the annual report and accounts prepared by the management and report on them.

The auditor is not responsible for preparing a company's financial statement or for maintaining its accounting records. His function is to give his professional opinion, after examination of the report and accounts, on whether or not they present a 'true and fair' picture of the company's financial position at the time the financial statement was prepared.

If he finds that he cannot confirm that the report and accounts are true and fair statement of the company's financial position, he is required to qualify his report so as to make it clear why he considers the report to be other than true and fair. In preparing his report, the auditor of a limited company is also required to judge whether proper accounting records have been kept by the company and whether the accounts presented to him for audit are consistent with those records.

An auditor is not primarily or specifically required to disclose errors, fraud or defalcations: the responsibility for detecting irregularities lies with the management of the company concerned.

To qualify for appointment as auditor, the person concerned must: (a) be a member of a recognised accountancy body; or (b) have been authorised by the Secretary of State, either as having obtained appropriate qualifications outside the United Kingdom or, having been employed by a member of a recognised body of accountants, be deemed to have acquired sufficient knowledge and experience. The bodies of accountants recognised by the Secretary of State are:

The Institute of Chartered Accountants in England and Wales

The Institute of Chartered Accountants in Scotland
The Association of Certified Accountants
The Institute of Chartered Accountants in Ireland

Bankruptcy

Virtually any individual can be made bankrupt. There are no exceptions for minors, married women, mental patients, MPs, peers or serving members of the armed forces. The estate of a deceased debtor may be made bankrupt.

Bankruptcy procedures have two main purposes:

(a) the equitable distribution of assets;
(b) a new start for the debtor.

However, the property subject to distribution does not include:

•   property held by debtor on trust;
•   tools of the trade of the debtor up to a value of £250;
•   goods subject to a seller's lien or to an unpaid seller's right of stoppage in transit;
•   retirement pensions;
•   property obtained by the debtor by mistake or fraud.

The court may order the debtor to make over to the trustee civil service pay, army or navy pay, salaries and copyright fees.

A debtor must not pay one creditor in preference to another. Payments made after the commencement of bankruptcy must be repaid to the trustee unless they were made in good faith in the ordinary course of business.

There are essential conditions to be fulfilled before a debtor can be made bankrupt.

•   The debtor was personally present in England at the time of the act of bankruptcy;
•   the debtor was ordinarily resident in England;
•   the debtor carried on business in England.

A British subject cannot be made bankrupt under English law if he is resident abroad.

Residence in Scotland is equivalent to residence abroad for the purposes of the English Bankruptcy Acts because there are separate (but similar) bankruptcy laws for Scotland.

An alien may be made bankrupt only if either he fulfills one of the conditions within one year of the start of proceedings or is domiciled in England.

The procedures

If the debtor has committed an act of bankruptcy, a creditor may petition the court for a receiving order. An act of bankruptcy is one of the following:

(a) notice of suspension of payment of debts;
(b) filing a declaration that debts cannot be paid;
(c) a judgment by any court of law followed by a seizure of the debtor's property by the sheriff;
(d) leaving or remaining out of England with the intention of defeating or delaying creditors;
(e) conveyance of debtor's property to a trustee for the benefit of creditors generally;
(f) fraudulent transfer of property;
(g) creation of a charge on property that amounts to a fraudulent preference.

When a receiving order is made, the control of the debtor's property passes to the Official Receiver.

The debtor must prepare a statement of affairs for creditors and attend a public examination. This is followed by a meeting of creditors which may:

(a) nominate a trustee or trustees to take over from the Official Receiver;
(b) appoint a Committee of Inspection to supervise the proceedings.

The duty of the trustee is to realise the estate and distribute the proceeds in the following sequence:

(a) expenses of realisation, including trustee's fee;
(b) pre-preferential debts (such as the funeral expenses if the debtor dies);
(c) preferential debts including local rates, income tax, wages and salaries of employees, national insurance contributions; preferential debts must be paid in full; if sufficient money is not available they must all be abated proportionally;
(d) ordinary debts in full if the assets are enough;
(e) deferred debts, if all the ordinary debts have been paid in full, namely:

(i) amounts due for goodwill purchased by the debtor;
(ii) loans made by one spouse to the other for business purposes.

A bankrupt may not act as director of a company; he may not operate a bank account.

To avoid these consequences, a debtor may seek a composition. This is an offer by the debtor to pay a proportion of the amount owing to each creditor in full satisfaction. If it is made before a receiving order, it binds only those creditors who consent. If it is made after the receiving order, the court must approve, and all creditors will then be bound.

Business letters

A company must show its name clearly on all of its business letters, notices and other publications, bills of exchange, promissory notes, endorsements, cheques and orders for money or goods, bills of parcels, invoices, receipts and letters of credit.

In addition, a company must show on its business letters and orders:

- place of registration;
- registered number;
- address of the registered office;
- if applicable, a statement that the company is an investment company;
- the fact that the company is a limited company if it is exempt from using the word 'limited' as part of its name;
- where there is any reference to share capital (not required by law but permitted), the reference must be to paid-up share capital;
- either the names, with initials or first names, of all of its directors or none; there is no requirement to state the nationality of directors;
- if a company is in liquidation, a statement to that effect must appear on its business letters, invoices or orders for goods;
- overseas companies carrying on business in Great Britain must give publicity to their name, country of incorporation and, where appropriate, the limited liability of the company.

Business names

The Business Names Act applies to any person who has a place of business in Great Britain (but not Northern Ireland) and who carries on a business under a name which:

(a) in the case of an individual, does not consist of his surname without any addition other than his forename or its initial;

(b) in the case of a partnership, does not consist of the surnames of all the partners who are individuals and the corporate names of all the partners who are corporate bodies without any addition other than the forenames of individual partners or the initials of those forenames or, where two or more individual partners have the same surname, the addition of 's' at the end of the surname;

(c) in the case of a company, does not consist of its corporate name without any addition.

For the purposes of the Act a 'company' is one that is subject to being wound up under the Companies Acts. This would include unregistered companies and overseas companies.

A person (... an individual, a partnership or a corporate body) to whom the Act applies must state his name and address in legible characters:

(a) on all business letters;

(b) on all written orders for the supply of goods or services to be supplied to the business;

(c) on all invoices and receipts issued in the course of business; and

(d) on all written demands for payment of debts arising in the course of business.

In the case of a partnership the name of each partner must be given. In the case of a company the corporate name must be given.

Written approval from the Secretary of State for Trade and Industry is required before a business may be carried on under a name which:

(a) would be likely to give the impression that the business is connected with the Government or with any local authority; or

(b) includes any word or expression for the time being specified in regulations made under the Act.

The following words and expressions require the permission of the Secretary of State for Trade and Industry before they may be used in a business name.

(a) Words which imply national or international pre-eminence:

British	Great Britain
England	National
English	Scotland
European	Scottish
Ireland	Wales
Irish	Welsh
International	United Kingdom

(b) Words which imply government patronage or sponsorship:

Authority Board Council

(c) Words which imply business pre-eminence or representative status:

Association	Institution
Federation	Society
Institute	

(d) Words which imply special objects or functions:

Assurance	Fund
Assurer	Giro
Benevolent	Holdings
Building Society	Industrial & Provident Society
Chamber of Commerce	Insurance
Chamber of Industry	Insurer
Chamber of Trade	Patent
Charter	Patentee
Chartered	Post Office
Chemist	Reassurance
Chemistry	Re-assurer

Co-operative	Register
Foundation	Registered
Friendly Society	Reinsurance
Reinsurer	Stock Exchange
Sheffield	Trade Union

(e) Words or expressions for which the opinion of a relevant body must be submitted:

Contact lens	Nurse
Dental	Nursing
Dentist	Police
District Nurse	Prince
Duke	Princess
Health Centre	Queen
Health Visitor	Royal
Her Majesty	Royale
His Majesty	Royalty
King	Special School
Midwife	Windsor
Midwifery	

The following are examples of words, the use of which is already restricted by legislation other than the Business Names Act.

Abortion	Drug
Anzac	Druggist
Apothecary	Dispensing optician
Architect	Enrolled optician
Architectural	Health service
Assurance broker	Insurance broker
Bank	Medical laboratory technician
Banker	Nursing home
Banking deposit	Occupational therapist
Breed	Opthalmic optician
Breeder	Optician
Breeding	Optometrist
Charitable	Orthopist
Charity	Pharmaceutical
Chiropodist	Pharmaceutist
Credit Union	Pharmacist
Dentist	Pharmacy
Dental practitioner	Physiotherapist
Dental surgeon	Polytechnic
Dietician	Pregnancy termination

Close companies

The term 'close company' was first introduced in the Finance Act of 1965 and the intention was to clarify the taxation liabilities of a family-owned company and its members. However, clarification of the taxation liabilities introduced considerable difficulties in determining whether or not a company is 'close'. In broad terms, a close company is one which is controlled either by (a) five or fewer participators or (b) by any number of participators who are directors. This definition requires two further definitions: of control and of participators.

Control is generally accepted to mean the ownership of most of the company's share capital; majority voting control or ownership of enough share capital to ensure that most of the income of the company, if distributed, would be received by the owner.

A participator is regarded as any person who receives, or is entitled to receive, benefits (income or assets) as a result of his connection with the company.

A close company owned by a family has its advantages, within the limits imposed by company law. It can, for example, distribute all of its profits to its participators; provide them with a wide range of benefits (accommodation, cars, etc); provide loans. But there are tax disadvantages for both a close company and its participators. For example, many of the payments or benefits to participators make them liable to tax. If the close company is not a trading company, company law requires that the whole or a proportion of its income must be distributed to its participators.

Co-operatives

Interest in co-operatives, dampened by a series of failures in the 1970s, has revived strongly in recent years. The new co-operatives are, in general, on a more modest scale than those of the last decade when the tendency was to form a worker's co-operative to carry on a business facing collapse in a changing economic climate.

In many cases failure reflected the fact that the original company's business was no longer viable in any case, irrespective of how it was conducted. A further factor was that some of the co-operatives were too ambitious in scale. Modern co-operatives, modest in scale and profiting from the lessons learned in the 1970s, are regarded as having a much better chance of success.

The essential principle behind the co-operative movement is the view that the members of an enterprise (workers, customers, producers, etc) have the right to the whole of the enterprise's success — financial and social — without having to give some of the profits to providers of capital.

Control is thus democratic — one member, one vote: profits are distributed in proportion to a member's particular dealings with the co-operative. In a consumer's co-operative, for example, the more a member buys, the greater his discount becomes in absolute terms.

The commonest legal structure for co-operatives is as industrial and provident societies. They differ from Friendly Societies, which are concerned with insuring members against various risks and which do not trade.

In theory — and sometimes in practice — a co-operative can adopt a partnership or company structure but, for many, either form may present problems. For example, a co-operative must be open for membership to anybody willing to accept membership responsibilities and who makes use of its services.

Partnership would thus be an unsuitable form of business structure for a co-operative with a large actual or potential membership, since there are legal restrictions on the number of partners permitted in many areas of work. Similarly, company law makes it a criminal offence for a private company to offer its shares for sale to the public. A consumer co-operative would thus not be able to advertise for new members, if operating as a company.

Companies and their formation

Any two or more people, associated for a lawful purpose, may form a company, with or without limited liability.

Their liability may be:

(a) limited by the amount, if any, unpaid on the shares they hold (a company limited by shares);
(b) limited to such amounts as they may agree to contribute to the assets if the company is wound up (limited by guarantee); or
(c) with no limit (unlimited company).

The company may be public or private. A public company is a company limited by shares or limited by guarantee and having a share capital, whose memorandum of association states that it is to be a public company.

A private company is one that is not a public company: a private company may not invite the public to buy its shares. The name of a public company must end with the words 'public limited company' (plc) or its equivalent in Welsh — 'cwmni cyfyngedig cyhoeddus'. A private company limited by shares or by guarantee must have the word 'limited' (cyfyngedig) as the last word in its company name. A company whose memorandum of association states that no dividends will be paid to its members and whose profits or income will be applied to promoting its objects (charities, professional bodies, for example) may be exempted from including 'limited' as the last word in its name.

A public company, if registered as such on incorporation, may not do business or borrow money until the Registrar of Companies has issued a certificate that the company complies with the minimum capital requirements (currently £50,000). A public company:

- must not pay a dividend if the net assets are less than the called-up share capital and undistributable reserves;
- must have at least two directors;
- must not appoint at a general meeting more than one director in a single resolution, except with the unanimous approval of the meeting;
- must call a general meeting if the value of net assets falls below half of the called-up share capital.

Registration

The Registrar of Companies issues a Certificate of Incorporation after receiving and approving:

- Memorandum of association;
- Articles of association;
- Statement of proposed capital;
- Declaration of compliance with the requirements of the Companies Acts;
- Statement of registered office;
- Statement of directors and secretary; and
- for public companies only, application for Certificate of Compliance with Share Capital Requirements.

Memorandum of Association

The form and contents of a memorandum of a public company are to be as follows:

- The name of the company is XXX.
- The company is to be a public company.
- The registered office of the company will be situated in (England or Wales) (Scotland).
- The objects for which the company is established are: XXXXXXXXX.
- The liability of the members is limited.
- The share capital of the company is divided into x shares of £x each.

We, the subscribers to this memorandum, wish to be formed into a company pursuant to this memorandum: and we agree to take the number of shares shown opposite our respective names.

Names, addresses of subscribers	Number of shares taken by each
Dated day of 19	subscriber
	Total shares taken

....   Witness to the above

Essential Facts for Managers

A private company would omit clause 2. Only two subscribers are necessary and usually each will subscribe for only one share.

Stamp duty (currently £1 per cent) is payable on the amount of nominal capital and the Statement of Capital filed with the Registrar must bear the appropriate stamp showing that the duty has been paid.

Articles of Association

The Articles outline the regulations proposed for the management of the company. They must include details of share capital, transfer or transmission of shares, general meetings, powers and duties of directors, dividends, the accounts and the annual audit.

The Articles must be divided into paragraphs numbered consecutively, stamped and signed by each subscriber to the memorandum in the presence of at least one witness. The Articles bind both members and company, but only in matters in which the members are concerned as members: they do not give rights to non-members. A company may subsequently alter its Articles by a special resolution of its members, but the alteration must be in good faith and for the benefit of the company as a whole.

A company will be private on registration unless the Memorandum of Association specifically states it is to be public. A public company, if registered as such on incorporation, must not do business or borrow money until the Registrar of Companies has issued a certificate that the company complies with the minimum capital requirements (currently £50,000). A public company may re-register as private and vice versa. A private company may not invite the public to buy its shares.

Dividends

- The directors decide the amount of a dividend to be paid, if any, and the annual general meeting must pass a resolution for the payment. The directors may recommend a dividend only out of realised profits, less realised losses from previous years.
- A dividend is not permissible if payment would result in the company being unable to pay its debts.
- No provision need be made for depreciation on fixed assets; losses of circulating capital must be written off.
- A dividend may be paid out of realised profits from the sale of fixed assets if a revaluation of remaining assets shows a surplus.
- An unrealised surplus on a revaluation of all assets may not be used to pay a dividend, but may be used to issue bonus shares if the Articles permit.
- A public company may pay dividends only to the extent of the excess of net assets over called-up share capital and undistributable reserves.

154

- If a dividend is paid improperly, it must be repaid to the company by any shareholder who received it, knowing, or having reasonable grounds to know, that legal requirements had not been met.

Company meetings

- Each company must hold an Annual General Meeting (AGM) in each calendar year.
- As long as a company holds its first AGM within 18 months of its incorporation, it need not hold one in the year of its incorporation or in the following year.
- Not more than 15 months may elapse between two consecutive AGMs.
- If default is made in complying with the above requirements, any member of the company may apply to the Department of Trade and Industry, which may direct the meeting to be called.
- Where such a meeting is not held in the year in which the default occurred, it will not be treated as the AGM for the year in which it is held unless a resolution that it shall be so treated is passed at the meeting.
- The annual return must be made up to the 14th day after the AGM for the year and completed within 42 days of the meeting and sent to the Registrar of Companies.

All general meetings other than AGMs are called Extra-ordinary General Meetings (EGMs).

- The directors are normally given power in the Articles to convene an ECM whenever they think fit.
- The directors *must* convene an EGM on the requisition of:

  (i) members holding at least 10 per cent of such paid-up capital as carries the right of voting; or

  (ii) where there is no share capital, members representing at least 10 per cent of total voting rights.

The requisition must:

  (i) state the objects of the meeting;
  (ii) be signed by the requisitionists; and
  (iii) be deposited at the company's registered office.

- The directors must also convene an EGM on requisition by a resigning auditor, who has made a statement of the circumstances connected with his resignation, which he considers should be brought to the attention of the company.

  If the directors do not proceed to convene a meeting, to be held within 28 days after the date of the notice, within 21 days after the deposit of the requisition, every director who failed to take all reasonable steps to do so is liable to a fine.

155

Company names

The name of a company must end either in 'limited' (for private companies) or 'public limited company'; or their abbreviations — Ltd and plc. When the company's registered office is in Wales, the Welsh equivalents may be used: Cyfyngedig (Cyf) and Cwmnicyfyngedig (Ccc).

When the Welsh terms are used and the company is a public limited company, that fact must be stated in English on bills, letter paper and other publications and at every place where the company carries on business.

A company must not adopt a name:

1   the same as a name already in the index of names kept by the Registrar of Companies, or which the Secretary of State for Trade and Industry considers to be offensive, or the use of which would, in the opinion of the Secretary of State, constitute a criminal offence;
2   that gives the impression that the company is connected with the government or any local authority;
3   that includes any word or expression designated in regulations made by the Secretary of State.

The name of a company must be shown conspicuously on the outside of every place of business of the company and stated in all business letters and documents. It must also be engraved on the company's seal.

Once formed, a change of name requires a special resolution by the company's shareholders; a change may also be directed by the Secretary of State.

The Registrar of Companies maintains company records for England and Wales at:

> Crown Way,
> Maindy,
> Cardiff CP4 3UZ
> Tel: 0222-388588

for Scotland at:

> Exchequer Chambers,
> George Street,
> Edinburgh EH2 3DJ
> Tel: 031-225 5774

and for Northern Ireland records are kept by:

> Department of Commerce,
> Chichester House,
> Chichester Street,
> Belfast PT1 3JX
> Tel: 0232-34121

Company records

Each company is required to keep accounting records which show and explain the company's transactions in a form which:

(a) shows, with reasonable accuracy, the company's financial position at the time;
(b) enables the directors to ensure that any balance sheet and profit and loss account can be properly prepared in conformity with the requirements of the Companies Acts.

In particular, the accounting records must contain a daily record of the company's receipts and expenditures and a record of the company's assets and liabilities. Where a company's business involves dealing in goods, the records must also contain a statement of stock held by the company at the end of each financial year and a statement of stocktakings from which stock figures have been prepared.

The statutory accounts (annual financial statements) which a company distributes to its shareholders for their approval must contain:

* the directors' report;
* the auditors' report;
* balance sheet;
* profit and loss account;
* notes showing the accounting policies used in preparing the accounts, share capital, particulars of allotments of shares, particulars of debts, basis on which any foreign currency sums have been converted to sterling and corresponding amounts for the previous financial year.

Companies resolutions

Special resolution

One passed by at least 75 per cent of the members who, being entitled to vote, do so in person or by proxy (where allowed), at a general meeting of which at least 21 days' notice, specifying the intention to propose the resolution, has been duly given.

Extraordinary resolution

One passed by at least 75 per cent of the members who, being entitled to vote, do so in person or by proxy (where allowed), at a general meeting of which notice specifying the intention to propose the resolution as an extraordinary resolution has been duly given.

Ordinary resolution

Any other resolution.

Essential Facts for Managers

Special or extraordinary resolutions

The following are the cases in which a special or extraordinary resolution is required. For all other purposes an ordinary resolution is sufficient.

Special resolution

- Alter the objects in the Company's Memorandum.
- Alter the Articles.
- Alter any provision in the Memorandum which could lawfully have been in the Articles.
- Determine that uncalled capital shall be called only in a winding-up.
- Reduce the company's capital (subject to confirmation by the court).
- Alter Memorandum to render liability of directors or managers or any managing director unlimited.
- Approve assignment of the office of director.
- Resolve that a company be wound up by the court or voluntarily.
- In a voluntary winding-up, sanction the acceptance of shares as consideration for the sale of property.
- Re-register a private company as public.
- Re-register a public company as private.
- Change a company's name.
- Approve the giving of financial assistance by a private company in certain circumstances in connection with the acquisition of shares in itself or its holding company.
- In connection with the purchase of a company's own shares, authorise the terms of:

  (a) a contract for an off-market purchase;
  (b) a contingent contract; or
  (c) an agreement for the release by a company of rights of purchase of its own shares.

- Approve the purchase or redemption of a company's own shares out of capital.
- Alteration of the nominal capital, unless the Articles permit this to be done by ordinary resolution.

Extraordinary resolution

- Resolve that a company cannot, by reason of its liabilities, continue its business and that it is advisable to wind up.
- Sanction in a members' voluntary winding-up the exercise of certain powers by the liquidator or an arrangement with creditors.
- Direct in a members' voluntary winding-up the way in which the books and papers of the company and of the liquidator may be disposed of.
- Sanction in a winding-up the division of assets among members in specie.
- Do anything else which, by a company's Articles, requires an extraordinary

resolution (other than something for which the Companies Acts require a special resolution).

Variation of the rights of a class of shares also usually requires the passing of an extraordinary resolution at a separate meeting of shareholders of that class.

Data Protection Act

In general, the Act applies to any person (or company) who holds personal data and requires that person to register with the Data Protection Register.

'Personal data' is data relating to a living individual, from which he can be identified and includes expressions of opinion (such as an indication of credit-worthiness).

The Act refers to a 'data user' but this is not meant to include the use of some data base such as Prestel. Within the meaning of the Act, a data user is someone who has personal data on file and processes it, updates, amends or extracts information from it.

The Act establishes a Data Registrar and makes it an offence to keep files of personal information that have not been registered and to make unauthorised use of personal data. It also:

- requires the Registrar to accept or refuse an application for registration as soon as possible and within six months at the latest;
- requires the Registrar to make the Register available to the public;
- empowers the Registrar to prohibit the transfer of data out of the UK;
- makes it an offence for a computer bureau to disclose personal data without authority;
- gives powers to enter and inspect when contravention of the Acts is suspected;
- imposes liability on directors and other officers of companies;
- entitles an individual to be informed by a data user whether personal data is held and to be given a copy;
- gives an individual right to compensation for damages and stress arising from inaccurate data;
- allows compensation for loss of data or for its unauthorised disclosure.

The Act exempts data used purely for payroll, accounting, pension and financial forecasting purposes.

Personal data stored on file must be obtained lawfully and fairly and may not be used for other than the purposes specified in the registration.

Directors

A private company must have at least one director. A public company registered on or after November 1929 must have at least two: a public company registered before that date need have only one. Every company must have a secretary; a sole director may not also be the secretary.

A company may be a director or secretary of another company. However, no company may have as its secretary a corporation, the sole director of which is the sole director of the company; nor may a company have as its sole director a corporation, the sole director of which is secretary to the company.

The directors of a public company must take all reasonable steps to ensure that the secretary has the requisite knowledge and experience to discharge the functions of secretary of the company.

Retirement

Directors must retire by rotation and may vacate office in certain events (see below). Where the company's Articles of Association give a director the power of assigning his office (which is very unusual), such an assignment must be sanctioned by a special resolution.

Except in limited circumstances, a director must vacate office at the end of the Annual General Meeting starting after he reaches 70. The rule is subject to the following points.

- It applies only to public companies and to private companies which are either subsidiaries of public companies or registered in Northern Ireland as public companies.
- No provision for automatic re-appointment will apply; if, at the meeting at which he retires, the vacancy is not filled, it may be filled by a casual vacancy.
- The rule will not apply if the director's appointment is or was made or approved by the company in general meeting. Special notice is required and the notice to and by the company must state or must have stated the age of the relevant person.
- A person appointed or proposed to be appointed a director is obliged to inform the company if he has attained the age of 70 or any other retiring age under the company's Articles.

Removal

A company may by ordinary resolution remove a director before the end of his period of office, notwithstanding anything in its Articles or in any agreement between the company and the director. This does not apply to a director of a private company who held office for life on 18 July 1948.

Special notice is required of any resolution to remove a director or to appoint somebody instead of him at the meeting at which he is removed.

As soon as notice is received to remove a director, the company must send a copy of it to the director, who is entitled to be heard at the meeting.

The director may make representations in writing and request that they be notified to the members. The company must, if it is not too late, state in the notice of resolution that representations have been made, and send a copy of the representations to every member to whom notice had been sent unless, on the application of the company or an aggrieved person, a court decides they are defamatory. If a copy is not sent, because the notice was received too late or because of the company's default, the director may require the representations to be read out at the meeting.

If a vacancy created by the removal of a director is not filled at the meeting at which he is removed, it may be filled as a casual vacancy.

Where a director is removed under this procedure, he is not thereby deprived of any compensation or damages otherwise payable in respect of the termination of his appointment.

Disqualification

- An undischarged bankrupt may not act as a director, except with the leave of the court which adjudged him bankrupt.
- The court may make a disqualification order restraining persons convicted of certain offences or who have been persistently in default in filing documents, from being directors, liquidators, receivers or otherwise involved in the promotion, formation or management of a company.
- A similar disqualification order may be made against a person who has been a director of two or more companies which have gone into liquidation within five years, if it appears to a court that the director's conduct as director of any of those companies makes him unfit to be concerned in the management of the company.
- The maximum duration of a disqualification order is fifteen years, or five years where the order is made by a court of summary jurisdiction, or for persistent default in filing documents.

The company's Articles may provide for certain circumstances in which directors become disqualified. Typically, these are:

- if he ceases to be a director because he has not obtained his share qualification or, because he is over the age limit;
- if he becomes bankrupt or makes any arrangement or composition with his creditors generally;
- if he becomes prohibited because of a court order;
- if he suffers from mental disorder and certain orders are made against him;
- if he resigns his office by notice to the company.

Fair dealing by directors

In general, company law lays upon the directors of a company the duty to manage that company with proper skill, diligence and care and to act in good faith, not to make improper use of company property and not to gain an improper advantage at the expense of the company. This duty is owed to the company and not to individual members of it.

The relevant sections of the Companies Acts carry a number of provisions designed to enforce fair dealings by directors.

- A company may not pay a director remuneration calculated as being free of income tax. A director receiving such a payment will be taxed on the net sum actually received.
- Shareholders' approval is required before payment may be made to a director for loss of office or on retirement.
- A director who has an interest, direct or indirect, in any contract or other agreement which his company is contemplating, or has contemplated, with another company must declare those interests as soon as possible.
- A copy of each director's contract of service (or a written memorandum setting out the terms of a contract of service which is not in writing) must be kept either at the company's registered office or at its normal place of business. The company must make provision enabling any shareholder in the company to inspect the contracts in periods of not less than two hours each day.
- A resolution of the company in its annual general meeting is required to approve a director's contract of employment which is for a period of more than five years and which (a) the company cannot end by giving notice or (b) can be ended only in specified circumstances.
- A resolution of the company's shareholders is required to approve any arrangement whereby a director acquires non-cash assets of a company, except where the value of the non-cash assets is below £1,000 or, if over £1,000, does not exceed £50,000 or 10 per cent of the company's asset value.
- Anyone becoming a director of a company must notify the company in writing of any interest he may have in the company's shares or debentures. This provision applies to the wife or husband of a director and to children. If the company's shares are listed on a recognised stock exchange, the company must notify the stock exchange of the director's interest.
- A company may not make a loan to a director, or provide security or guarantee for a loan to a director. The provision includes quasi-loans — payments made to a third party on behalf of a director. It does not include small loans of up to £2,500 in aggregate.

Directors' duties

- To manage the company in accordance with its Articles of Association, using their powers for a proper purpose and for the company's benefit.

* To act with the skill reasonably to be expected from a person of the director's knowledge and experience.
* To avoid any conflict of interest.
* To use company assets solely for company purposes.

The board

The powers and duties of a board of directors are determined by the company's Articles. Most companies have Articles similar to a set of model articles in the Companies Act.

* Directors may arrange their meetings as they wish; decisions are taken by a majority of directors present at a meeting.
* Unless the directors decide otherwise, the quorum necessary at a meeting for the transaction of business is two directors personally present.
* If the number of directors entitled to be present at a meeting falls below the number fixed by the Articles, the remaining directors may only elect new directors or summon a shareholders' meeting.
* Directors should elect from among themselves a chairman; if no election is made, or the elected chairman is not present within five minutes of the appointed time for the meeting, the directors present may choose one of their number to be chairman at that meeting.
* Directors may delegate any of their powers to a member, or a committee of the board.
* A written resolution signed by all directors is as valid as if it had been passed at a board meeting.

General meetings

Directors must summon a general meeting of shareholders once each calendar year to consider the company's accounts and directors' report, and to elect directors and the auditor. Subject to the Articles, they may call an extraordinary general meeting whenever they think fit: in the case of a public company, they *must* call a meeting if its net assets fall in value to one-half or less of the amount of the called-up share capital.

The directors must call a meeting of shareholders at the request of retiring auditors, or on the requisition of shareholders holding one-tenth of the voting shares. If the directors fail to act within 21 days, the requisitioning shareholders have three months in which to call a meeting themselves. One director or two shareholders may convene a meeting if no quorum of directors is present in the United Kingdom.

Non-executive directors

Company law does not require a director of a company to hold shares in that company; neither does it give a director the right, simply because he is a director, of being paid for his directorship. In practice and in general, the trend is for companies not to require their directors to own shares, and to pay them a regular salary, under the terms of a contract of service. Such directors are, in effect, full-time employees of their company and are subject to those requirements of company law affecting directors.

Full-time salaried directors are commonly known as executive directors with the authority to take decisions and exercise control within whatever area of administration and management the board may have allocated to them. In many of the larger companies, it is common for all directors to be salaried and executive. But companies are free to have boards made up of both executive directors and directors who are paid a fee to attend meetings and give their advice and opinions, but who have no executive powers within the company.

The appointment of a non-executive director with specialist knowledge, experience or extensive personal contacts in a particular field of business has considerable attractions for smaller companies.

Insider dealing

The Companies Acts prohibit:

- dealing in shares of a company by a person connected with the company having price-sensitive information;
- dealing in shares of a company by a person connected with another company when a take-over has been contemplated;
- dealing in shares of a company by a person who has acquired information from a person connected with that company;
- dealing in shares of companies by a person who has unpublished, price-sensitive information about a possible take-over.
- procuring or counselling another person to deal in shares by a person who has unpublished information;
- communicating price-sensitive information to a person likely to make use of it.

Insolvency

Insolvency is normally taken to mean an inability to pay creditors in full within a reasonable time — 12 months, in general — and is commonly applied both to companies and individuals. In more precise terms, an insolvent company faces winding-up; an insolvent individual faces bankruptcy.

A company finding itself unable to pay all its creditors in full within 12 months has no option: it must wind up its affairs. If it does not, a court can order it to do so and appoint somebody to see that it is done.

However, an insolvent company does have some limited choice in how its winding up is done. It can choose between calling in a liquidator and calling in a receiver. Appointment of a liquidator implies that the company has decided to cease trading completely since the liquidator's function is solely to realise the company's remaining assets for the benefit of the creditors. A receiver takes over the custody of the company's assets and does not necessarily realise them: he may, in appropriate circumstances, continue with the company's trade.

There is a further degree of choice for the insolvent company. Its directors, having decided the position is hopeless, can recommend a members' voluntary winding up to its shareholders. If the directors are a little slow in coming to this decision, the company's creditors, realising that things are not getting better, may elect to call a creditors' voluntary winding-up. If neither of these things happen, a court, responding to a petition by a creditor or group of creditors, may order a compulsory winding-up and appoint the Official Receiver to see that it is done. For the shareholders, directors and staff of a failed company, or for its creditors, none of the limited choices offers much comfort: the end result is much the same whatever the means of achieving it.

Order of settlement of liabilities

If the company is insolvent the claims must be settled in the following order:

(1) claims of secured creditors under a fixed charge, such as a bank loan;
(2) costs and expenses of administration;
(3) claims of preferential creditors;
(4) claims secured by a floating charge;
(5) claims of ordinary creditors;
(6) claims of employees;
(7) claims of the shareholders, e.g. unpaid dividends.

Each class of liability must be settled in full before paying subsequent classes.

Investor protection

The purpose of the Financial Services Act, 1986, is: 'to regulate the carrying on of investment business; to make related provision with respect to insurance business and business carried on by friendly societies; to make new provision with respect to the official listing of securities, offering of securities, take-over offers and insider dealing; to make provision for securing reciprocity with other countries with respect to facilities for the provision of financial services; and for connected purposes.'

The Act includes *inter alia*:

* definitions of investments and investment business;
* civil and criminal sanctions for unauthorised investment business;
* authorisation for self-regulation of investment business;
* powers to make rules and to authorise collective investment business (such as unit trusts);
* powers to disqualify persons from other countries carrying on investment business in the UK;
* provisions on official listing of securities; on contents of documents such as prospectuses, and on investigation of suspected insider dealing.

Liability

Company law is framed primarily to protect investors in particular, and the public in general, against malpractice and it imposes liabilities, some severe, on infringements. It is said that company law creates 80 or so offences and some of them carry prison sentences, on conviction, which can be as long as seven years, or more.

For example, a mis-representation in a prospectus inviting the public to buy shares or debentures in a company renders the person(s) concerned liable to be charged with a criminal offence and, on conviction, to serve a prison sentence. Failure to issue a prospectus when one is required under company law is also a criminal offence.

In general, company law imposes on the directors of a company the duty to ensure that its requirements are complied with. In some cases, the penalty for failing to comply with a particular requirement will be extracted from the company, not personally from the director(s) concerned. But the Acts contain many provisions which impose penalties for default on the directors as well as their companies. Failure to file an annual report in due time, for example, attracts a daily fine payable by both the company and its officers. In practice, the Department of Trade, which administers company law, is not aggressive in bringing prosecutions, except in flagrant cases of persistent default or fraud.

In general, company law lays upon directors the duty to act in good faith and with due care in the interests of the company and within the authority vested in them by the company. Ignorance of the requirements of company law is no defence against a prosecution, but if a director can prove that he did not knowingly and wilfully authorise a default, acting in good faith and within his authority, a court would be expected to take this into consideration.

A director who enters into a contract with an outside party and who, in so doing, acts within his authority is acting as his company's agent and invokes no personal liability for any action that may be brought as a consequence of the contract.

But he may be liable if he enters into a contract without disclosing his company's interest; if he signs a bill of exchange, a cheque or an order for money or goods without disclosing his company's name, he is personally liable if his company does not pay. If a director enters into a contract which, it later turns out, is beyond the powers either of himself or his company, he may be personally liable to a third party. An example might be the negotiation of a loan which is beyond his company's total borrowing limit.

Product liability

Perhaps because the numbers of injuries and deaths caused by defective products (including drugs) have been relatively small in the UK, product liability has not, hitherto, been a major factor for most British companies.

In the US the position is very different and, for several reasons, including the increasing complexity of products in general as well as the work of consumer pressure groups, product liability is becoming a much more important consideration for British companies.

Increasingly, security and safety are being built in to new products at the design stage. Under the stimulus of new legislation, much greater care is being taken with claims made for products. A side-effect of this legislation is that advertisements, particularly television commercials, now tend to be less specific in their claims.

A manufacturer of a product with a defect, which may or may not cause injury to the user or damage to his property, faces the possibility of legal liability for the consequences arising from the defect in three main situations.

- A Factory Inspector has the power to require the manufacturer of equipment used in a factory to make amendments to it if he considers that such amendments are needed to make the equipment safe to use. Failure to comply would be a criminal offence.
- A product that is defective in some way, without necessarily causing injury or damage to property, could attract an action under contract law. The user would claim, in such an action, that the product did not serve the purpose for which it was made because of the defect.
- A product with a defect causing injury to the user, or his property, may be liable in tort and damages awarded in such cases would be likely to be heavier than those imposed in a case based on contract law.

It is commonplace for manufacturers to insure against liability in tort, but not contract. Criminal liability is not insurable, apart from court and legal costs.

A case brought under contract law, where a product is claimed to be defective but not to have caused injury or damage, would be against the retailer selling the product to the user. If, in such an action, there was also a claim for damages, the user could claim only for injuries caused to himself, not for any third party.

An action in tort enables an injured party to bring the case against whomever was responsible for the defect causing the injury, and in favour of the person(s) suffering from it. Such an action has its restrictions. The plaintiff must prove first that the product was defective; that the defect caused the injury complained of; and that the defendant failed in his duty of care because the injury was a foreseeable consequence of the defect.

In everyday life, a consumer buying a defective product gets the retailer to change it. If the defect is in one item in an otherwise satisfactory production run, all is normally well. If, however, the defect is common to all items in the production run, legal action may result.

Liquidation

There is a clear distinction between liquidation and receivership:

- a company is placed in liquidation when it is considered necessary for it to cease trading and to realise the assets for the benefit of creditors and shareholders;
- receiverships involve placing a company's assets in the hands of a receiver who takes control and may continue to trade if circumstances permit.

There are three types of liquidation.

Members' (shareholders) voluntary winding-up

If a company's directors are able to declare that a company's liabilities can be met in full within a period of not more than 12 months from the date of a winding-up, the shareholders have the option of winding-up the company voluntarily.

Creditors' voluntary winding-up

If the company's liabilities cannot be paid in full within 12 months, the share-holders may still have the option of a voluntary winding-up but they will need the agreement of the company's creditors who may agree to a suitable division of the available assets.

Compulsory winding-up

A court may order a compulsory winding-up on presentation of a petition by the company, a creditor(s), the Official Receiver, the Department of Trade and Industry or the Attorney-General.

Partnerships

A partnership exists when two or more persons (which includes a company) carry on a business (which includes a profession) with the intention of making a profit (which means that a charity cannot be a partnership).

A partnership is presumed to exist when:

(a) property is owned in common or jointly;
(b) gross income from an enterprise is being shared;
(c) profits are shared.

This presumption may be contradicted by the circumstances and the Partnership Act 1980 specifically says that the presumption of the existence of a partnership does not arise merely when:

(a) a debt is paid by instalments out of profits;
(b) employees or agents are remunerated by a share of profits;
(c) payment for goodwill is made out of profits.

Partnerships normally come into existence by an agreement, which need not be written. The parties may not expressly state in words that they intend to form a partnership; their conduct may imply that they intended to be partners, so that the parties may unintentionally create a partnership by their conduct.

If the parties do not provide beforehand for unexpected events or contingencies, the provisions of the Partnership Act will apply. The results may not be what the partners want or intended.

Partners

Partners are described as:

(a) *General partners*, who may be fully active in the affairs of the firm, or *sleeping or dormant partners* who take no part in the partnership business but who are liable for the debts incurred by the active partners (not for debts incurred after their retirement, except when the creditor knew they had been partners and did not know of the retirement).
(b) *Limited partners*, who are liable only to the amount of capital they have undertaken to invest so long as they take no active part in the management of the firm.

Each partner is an agent in the partnership business of the firm and of the other partners. They have authority to:

(a) sell the goods and chattels of the partnership;
(b) receive and give a receipt for money owing;
(c) engage and dismiss employees.

In a trading firm they also have authority to:

(a) borrow money;
(b) issue or accept negotiable instruments.

The authority of a partner may be limited by the partnership agreement, but the limitation will bind only those persons who know of it. The authority is always limited to the business of the partnership. Other partners will not be bound if a partner enters into a transaction that is not connected with the partnership business.

Liability of a partner extends to all the debts and obligations of the partnership. Liability is joint for all liabilities arising under contract, which means a partner can be sued for a contract debt only in the name of the firm.

Each partner is fully liable for the whole of the firm's income tax liability.

In tort (example: professional negligence) liability is joint and several, which means a partner can be sued as an individual.

Private debts must be paid first out of a partner's private estate: the rest of the estate is liable for debts of the firm.

The Partnership Act

Rights and duties not set out in a partnership agreement are specified by the Partnership Act:

(a) All partners share equally in profits and losses;
(b) capital is contributed equally;
(c) no interest is payable on capital;
(d) no remuneration is payable on services;
(e) if one partner works more than others he is entitled only to an equal share in profits, except when the partnership agreement stipulates otherwise.

All partners must:

(a) take part in the management of the business;
(b) consent to the introduction of a new partner.

Consent must not be unreasonably withheld.

Decisions on ordinary matters connected with the business are decided by a majority vote.

Any change in the nature of the partnership business must be agreed by all partners.

Partnership books must be kept at the place of business of the firm; all partners have the right of access to books and records.

Each partner must give full information to his partners on all matters affecting the partnership, and must pay over all profits made in the course of the partnership business, and also profits made in any other business a partner has carried on without the consent of the other partners.

170

Ending a partnership

A partnership is ended by:

(a) agreement of the partners;
(b) death of a partner;
(c) bankruptcy of a partner (not of a limited partner);
(d) by the Court on application of a partner on grounds specified by the Partnership Act or under a general power to dissolve a partnership whenever the Court thinks dissolution would be just and equitable.

If a partnership is unable to pay its debts, each partner is liable to settle the firm's liabilities in full out of his own assets.

The Bankruptcy Act 1914 provides that, in a bankruptcy:

(a) partnership property must be used to pay partnership debts;
(b) separate property of a partner must first be used to pay his own debts;
(c) any surplus from separate estates is brought into the partnership estate;
(d) any surplus from the partnership is brought into the separate estates of the partners in proportion to the interest of each partner in the firm;
(e) any balance remaining after payment of separate and firm debts must be paid to the partners in accordance with the terms of the partnership agreement. If the agreement is silent on the point, the balance is divided equally.

Public and private companies

Company law requires that a company must be public or private, limited or unlimited. 'Limited' in this context means a company whose liabilities are limited either by the shares held by its members or the guarantees they undertake to give. (*See also*, Companies and their formation p.152.)

Public companies

A public company is a company limited by shares or limited by guarantee and having a share capital whose Memorandum of Association states that it is to be a public company and which has complied with the provisions of company law (Companies Act 1985) governing its registration (or re-registration) as a public company.

These provisions require that the company's Memorandum of Association is in a prescribed form. It must state:

1 The name of the company is *xxx*
2 The company is to be a public company
3 The registered office of the company will be situated in *xxx*

4   The objects for which the company is established are *xxx*
5   The liability of the members is limited
6   The share capital of the company is divided into *x* shares of £*y* each.

> We, the subscribers to this Memorandum, wish to be formed into a company pursuant to this Memorandum and we agree to take the number of shares shown against our respective names.

Only two subscribers are necessary to comply with the law and usually each will subscribe for only one share. Stamp duty (currently £1 per cent) is payable on the amount of nominal capital. The company's corporate name must end with the words public limited company (or plc) or their equivalents in Welsh.

Having complied with these requirements a public company may:

* offer its shares or debentures for sale to the public;
* allot such securities with a view to their being offered for sale to the public.

It is, however, subject to a number of restrictions:

* it must have a minimum share capital (currently £50,000) before it can do business or exercise any borrowing powers;
* it may not allot shares unless at least 25 per cent of the nominal value and the whole of any premium has been paid up;
* the original subscribers to its Memorandum must have paid in cash for the shares they have taken up;
* it may not distribute profits in the form of a dividend if its net assets are less than the total of its called-up share capital and its undistributable reserves;
* the directors must convene an extraordinary general meeting if the value of the company's net assets falls to 50 per cent or less of the amount of the called-up share capital;
* it may not name only one director on its business letters: it must either print the names and initials of all directors (individual and corporate) or none at all;
* it may not make loans (or quasi loans) to a director or anybody connected with a director except in limited and specified cases.

Private companies

A private company is simply a company that is not public. In forming its Memorandum of Association it would omit the clause (2 above) stating that the company was to be public. The essential difference from a public company is that a private one may not offer its shares to the public. To do so would be a criminal offence. A further difference is that it does not require a large amount of share capital and this makes a private company particularly suitable for small businesses and family concerns. (*See also*, Companies and their formation, p.152.)

Limited companies

A company, private or public, is required to pay all its debts while its assets as a corporate entity are sufficient to meet them. But the liability of its individual or corporate members is limited either by the shares they have bought or by guarantees they have given.

Thus, if a company becomes insolvent, shares in it become valueless and the investing member has lost the money paid for the shares. But he has no further liability for the company's debts.

For a company limited by guarantee the individual members' liability on insolvency ends when they have paid the amounts they have guaranteed to pay.

Formation as a company limited by guarantee is regarded as having advantages for clubs, societies, professional associations and similar groups whose members want to be incorporated without incurring personal liability.

Unlimited companies

Unlimited companies are relatively rare. Members are liable for any debts incurred by the company if it becomes insolvent, although these liabilities can be restricted.

An unlimited company does not need to have a share capital and, if it does not, it is not required to submit an annual return. As a form of incorporation an unlimited company has attractions for members wishing to keep its financial affairs secret.

Receivership

Receivership is a method whereby an agent (a receiver) is put in charge of a company's assets in order to secure repayment of an outstanding loan. The receiver may continue to trade (operating as receiver and manager) and his appointment does not necessarily mean that the company to which he is appointed is insolvent.

There are two main types of receivership — appointments under agreements and appointments by a court.

Appointments under agreements

The agreement gives power to another person to appoint a receiver to take custody of some or all of the assets on the occurrence of certain events.

It is usually entered into by a company (or an individual) wishing to borrow money, whereby the lender is given the right, if the borrower does not abide by the terms of the agreement, to appoint a receiver to take over assets to secure the repayment of the outstanding loan.

The agreement is called a charge, and may be either a 'fixed or legal charge' or a 'floating charge'.

A *fixed* charge relates to specific asset, e.g. land and buildings or book debts while *floating*:

(i)   covers any class of asset which constantly changes e.g. stock;
(ii) on the occurrence of certain events (usually the appointment of a receiver or the beginning of a liquidation), the charge crystallises and becomes 'fixed' over the assets in existence at that time;
(iii) is often combined with a 'fixed charge' in a 'fixed and floating charge'.

The most common agreement is the *debenture* secured by a charge, a debenture being an acknowledgement of indebtedness.

Appointments by the court

A judge in the High Court has power to appoint a receiver whenever it appears to the court that it is just and convenient for such an appointment to be made.

Applications for appointment may be made by a party to an action to protect the assets in the period before the action is tried or by secured creditors, where the company's assets have been pledged to secure a debt, but there is no power in the agreement for the creditor to appoint a receiver.

Who appoints the receiver?

- A creditor with a legal right to recover a debt out of assets.
- The court acting on behalf of a creditor or shareholder. The appointment must be made by deed or by court order. The appointment does not come into effect until the receiver or his agent has been notified of the appointment.

6 Civil and common law

Civil and common law

In broad terms, courts divide into two categories: those trying civil and those tying criminal cases. Civil law is concerned with helping individuals obtain redress for the harmful acts or omissions of others. Criminal proceedings may be brought only by the state, through any of its law enforcement agencies, and are designed to suppress crime and punish criminals.

Civil law provides for the recovery of losses suffered by an individual but does not impose a criminal penalty on those causing those losses. Criminal law punishes a convicted criminal but does not normally compensate his victim, although a criminal court can, and does, order compensation to be paid in certain circumstances.

The distinction between civil and criminal law is sometimes blurred. Much of criminal law is designed to protect the person and belongings of individuals: individuals and the state share common interests. However, it is a principle of English law that a court is required to take judicial notice of the whole of law so that the essential differences between civil and criminal law lie in the proceedings involved.

A sub-division of civil law allows the possibility of treating a harmful act or omission as either a tort (wrong) or a breach of contract, or both. Alternate claims may be heard in the same action but the court will award only a single amount of damages.

Where no personal injury is involved and the cases concern only redress arising from failure to honour a contract, or to honour it imperfectly, a case for breach of contract might be the simplest procedure. It would almost certainly be quicker since no action in tort is, in general, more complex.

Straddling all forms of law is common law. It is a very substantial body of law built on commonsense findings of courts over a long period, and its essential feature is that it is based on precedents. Because it takes regard of previous court decisions in cases similar to one being tried, it tends to be rigid. A decision based on common law cannot be reversed, except by a higher court. This is not easily done since a precedent, provided it is still relevant in principle, does not lose any authority simply because it is old.

Underlying all law is the principle that it must be consistent. If two separate courts give two different decisions in similar cases, either in different parts of the country or at different times, the argument is that one of them must be wrong, if circumstances have not changed.

The courts

- Civil cases are heard by local county courts and by the High Court in London and other large cities: appeals are heard by the civil division of the Court of Appeal.

- Criminal cases involving a jury are tried by Crown Courts: appeals go to the criminal division of the Court of Appeal.
- Summary criminal cases are tried by magistrates' courts, with appeals to a Crown Court or a Divisional Court.
- The House of Lords is the final court of appeal for all cases.

Cheques

A cheque is a type of negotiable instrument, which is defined as: 'an unconditional order in writing, addressed by one person to another, requiring the person to whom it is addressed to pay on demand or at a fixed or determinable future time a sum certain in money to or to the order of a specified person or to bearer'.

The bank must not pay a cheque when:

(a) the customer has countermanded payment;

(b) the bank has received notice that the customer has been declared mentally incapable;

(c) the bank has received notice that the customer has committed an act of bankruptcy on which a petition could be based;

(d) a receiving order has been made against the customer;

(e) in the case of a company, winding-up proceedings have been commenced;

(f) the bank knows that there is a defect in the title of the person presenting the cheque for payment or that the customer has drawn the cheque in breach of trust or for some unlawful purpose;

(g) the bank has received notification of the death of the customer.

When a cheque is crossed, payment must not be made over the counter, but to another bank or to another account in the same bank.

(a) The customer may indicate on the crossing that payment is to be made only to a named bank.

(b) A crossing with the words 'account payee only' imposes on the collecting bank the obligation to ensure that it is collecting on behalf of the proper payee.

(c) The holder may add to an endorsement but cannot change any previous endorsement.

Close seasons

Taking or killing game birds is illegal:

• for grouse or red game	December 10 – August 12
• for black game	December 10 – August 20

- for partridges   February 1 – September 1
- for pheasants   February 1 – October 1

It is also an offence to take or kill game on Sundays or on Christmas Day. The killing or taking of game, wild birds and the eggs of birds is subject to extensive legislation and, in general, specific authorisation is required.
Some points are:

- hares (or leverets) may not be sold during March, April, May, June or July, except for foreign hares imported for sale;
- the cage of a captive bird must be large enough to enable it to stretch its wings freely;
- swans are 'royal fowl' and whales and sturgeons are 'royal fish': if they are not lawfully owned by some private person they belong to the Queen;
- anyone is free to fish on the high seas and tidal waters (including estuaries) up to the high water level, provided nobody has ownership or other rights in a particular area;
- it is illegal to take, kill or own any freshwater fish which is about to spawn, or which has not recovered from a recent spawning;
- it is illegal to take a salmon of less than 12 inches in length.

Copyright

The basic principle underlying copyright law is that ideas are free for anyone to use, but a person's expression of his ideas is his own property.

Unlike a patent or a trade mark, copyright cannot be registered. Protection for copyright holders is contained in three Acts, the Copyright Act of 1956 and two Performers Protection Acts. Authors, composers of musical works and artists all have rights in the work they produce and can control reproduction in any form. Similarly, a performer of any kind, whose performance is artistic in nature, is protected in law against the unauthorised reproduction of the performance in any form. Copyright law extends its protection to those who, with the agreement of the originator, reproduce original work: they — publishers, film producers, recording companies, etc — have rights in their reproduction.

The intention of the appropriate Acts is clear: anyone reproducing material from a copyright work without authorisation risks a legal action. A private recording by a private person in his own home for his personal use of a copyright work is unlawful; it is, however, accepted that enforcement of the law on this point is virtually impossible. The Acts do, however, allow some copying. A critic reviewing a book may reasonably quote extracts from that book; a student preparing for an examination may copy extracts from a text book. Copyright protection extends for the life of the originating author, composer or artist, plus 50 years. Thereafter, the provisions of the Copyright Act do not apply.

Divorce

The three main courses open to a couple in a matrimonial suit are:

- divorce: the marriage tie is dissolved and, after a *decree nisi* becomes absolute, either party may re-marry;
- judicial separation: the marriage tie remains, but the couple are not required to co-habit and, if one partner dies intestate, the property of the deceased partner devolves as if the other partner were already dead;
- nullity: the marriage is declared null and void.

The sole ground for divorce is that the marriage has broken down irretrievably: no such ground need to be shown for judicial separation.

However, in both cases, the court must be satisfied on one or more of the following points:

(a) the respondent has committed adultery and the petitioner finds it intolerable to live with the respondent;

(b) the respondent has behaved in such a way that the petitioner cannot reasonably be expected to live with the respondent;

(c) the respondent has deserted the petitioner for a continuous period of at least two years immediately preceding presentation of the petition;

(d) the parties to the marriage have lived apart for a continuous period of at least two years immediately preceding presentation of the petition and the respondent consents to a decree being granted;

(e) the parties to the marriage have lived apart for a continuous period of at least five years immediately preceding presentation of the petition.

Nullity

Grounds for nullity depend on whether the marriage is alleged to be void (regarded as never having taken place) or voidable (valid until annulled).

Marriages celebrated after 31 July, 1971 are void if:

(a) the parties are within the prohibited degrees of relationship (see below); or

    (i)   either party is under the age of 16; or

    (ii) the parties have intermarried in disregard of certain requirements as to the formation of marriage;

(b) at the time of marriage either party was already lawfully married;

(c) the parties are not respectively male or female;

(d) in the case of polygamous marriage entered into outside England and

Wales, either party was at the date of marriage domiciled in England and Wales.

Voidable marriages

Marriages celebrated after 31 July, 1971 are voidable if:

(a) the marriage has not been consummated owing to the incapacity of either party;

(b) the marriage has not been consummated owing to the wilful refusal of the respondent;

(c) either party to the marriage did not validly consent to it, whether in consequence of duress, mistake, unsoundness of mind or otherwise;

(d) at the time of marriage the respondent was suffering from venereal disease in a communicable form and the petitioner was ignorant of that fact;

(e) at the time of marriage either party, though capable of giving a valid consent, was suffering from a mental disorder of such a kind or to such an extent as to be unfitted for marriage;

(f) at the time of marriage the respondent was pregnant by some person other than the petitioner who was ignorant of that fact.

Evidence

Rules governing the admissibility of evidence are virtually the same in both criminal and civil cases. However, in a civil action, a decision may be reached on the preponderance of probability. A criminal action requires a decision based on proving the charge against the defendant with certainty. Evidence falls into two main categories: primary and secondary. The former, in practice, means the best available, such as an eye-witness's account of an event.

The second implies that better evidence may exist but is not available. A witness is always required to give evidence orally, but may refer to notes made at the time or immediately afterwards. Hearsay evidence is not generally accepted, although there are exceptions in particular circumstances. There are also exceptions to the general rule that neither husband nor wife may give evidence for or against each other.

A free and voluntary confession of guilt, made without any suggestion of duress or of being obtained by direct or implied promises, is regarded as the highest and most satisfactory proof.

Firearms

A certificate, obtainable from the police, is required for the lawful purchase, acquisition or possession of any firearm, including a shot-gun.

No certificate is required for most airguns (but there are exceptions), but nobody under 14 may possess an airgun unless:

(a) he/she is supervised by somebody aged 21 or over; and
(b) uses the airgun on private premises and does not shoot at any target outside those premises.

Injunctions

The main factor governing the award of an injunction is that damages would not be an adequate remedy for the plaintiff in the case.

In general, but not invariably, injunctions are awarded to prevent the continuance of some action complained of (such as an infringement of a registered trade mark). An injunction requiring positive action by the defendant may be made, but only if this would not require the continued supervision of a court.

It is open to a plaintiff to seek an interlocutory injunction which, in effect, is an interim ruling in force only until the action is heard. A plaintiff seeking an interlocutory injunction may be required to provide an undertaking to pay damages to the defendant if, at the subsequent hearing, it is established that the interlocutory injunction should not have been granted. A further option is to seek an *ex parte* injunction, where the defendant does not appear. Such injunctions are usually awarded for short periods only.

Intestacy

When there is a surviving spouse

If there is issue:

(a) surviving spouse receives £40,000 and personal chattels absolutely;
(b) one-half of balance of estate to be on statutory trusts for issue but spouse to receive income;
(c) other half to be on statutory trusts for issue.

If there is no issue, but surviving parent or brother or sister (or their issue):

(a) surviving spouse receives £85,000, personal chattels and one-half of balance;
(b) other half of residue goes to parent absolutely, or if no surviving parent, on statutory trusts for brothers and sisters.

Surviving spouses may require the transfer of the family house as part of their share.

When there is no surviving spouse

If there is issue:

• the whole estate is to be held on statutory trusts for issue.

If there is no issue, but parents:

• parents receive the whole estate.

If there are relatives but no parents or issue:

• relatives take the whole estate in the following order:

    (i)   brothers and sisters or their issue of the whole blood;
    (ii) brothers and sisters of the half blood or their issue;
    (iii) grandparents in equal shares;
    (iv) uncles and aunts of the whole blood or their issue;
    (v) uncles and aunts of the half blood or their issue.

If there are no relatives:

• the whole estate falls as ownerless property to the Crown, Duchy of Lancaster or Duchy of Cornwall.

Juries

With the exceptions listed below, anyone is liable for jury service, who:

(a) is between 18 and 65;
(b) is on parliamentary or local electoral rolls; and
(c) has lived in the United Kingdom, the Channel Islands or the Isle of Man for any period of at least five years since reaching the age of 13.

The exceptions are:

(a) anybody who has been sentenced to three months' imprisonment or more in the 10 years preceding a call for jury service;
(b) anybody who has ever been sentenced to life imprisonment or for five years or more;
(c) anybody who holds or has held judicial office, or is concerned with the administration of justice;
(d) ministers of any religious denomination;
(e) members and officers of parliament;
(f) full-time serving members of the armed forces;
(g) practising members of the medical professions, including nurses and mid-wives.

Jurors are entitled to payment (at prescribed scales) for travelling and subsistence costs, loss of earnings and any other costs reasonably incurred as a result of being called to serve. A person summoned to serve, but not sworn, is entitled to payment. Anyone summoned for jury service who fails to attend as directed is subject to a fine unless he qualifies for the exceptions listed above or:

(a) can show that he has already served on a jury within the two years preceding a further call to service;
(b) can show that the summons requiring him to attend was served less than 14 days before the date of required attendance.

The jury's duty is to determine questions of fact based on admissible evidence placed before it. It is the judge's duty to decide on questions of admissability of evidence. If there is no admissible evidence, the judge must direct the jury accordingly. He is free to express personal opinions (as distinct from explaining a legal point) but, if he does so, he must make it clear to the jury that they need not accept them.

A jury has absolute power to convict or acquit in criminal cases, or to find a verdict for either the plaintiff or defendant in civil cases. This applies even where the verdict may appear to be contrary to the evidence or to the direction given by the judge.

Jury trials in civil actions have decreased in number: in crown courts, a trial by jury is mandatory if the defendant pleads not guilty.

Libel

A libel is generally held to be anything published (printed or written) or broadcast (radio or television) which holds a person up to hatred, contempt or ridicule.

To be actionable, a libel does not have to be intentional, nor does it necessarily have to be directed at a particular person. The law is concerned with whom was injured by a libel, and not with what was meant by the defamatory statement complained of. The law also requires the plaintiff to establish that the defamatory statement complained of was published to a third party. Thus, a libellous statement in a sealed letter to somebody who might reasonably be expected to open the letter personally, would be unlikely to be actionable: it would not be seen as being published to a third party.

But a letter which might reasonably be opened by the addressee's secretary might, if libellous, be actionable: so might a libel written on a postcard, since it could be seen by the postal officers handling it.

A news vendor or bookseller who, in the normal course of business, unknowingly sells a publication containing a libellous statement, would not normally be liable to an action for libel. Admissible defence against a libel action may include any of the following.

• It was fair comment and made with public interest in mind.
• It was true.

- It was unintentional and an apology has been made.
- It was a privileged statement.

A privileged statement may be made:

- in court during judicial proceedings;
- in an accurate newspaper report of those proceedings;
- in the Houses of Parliament;
- in parliamentary papers;
- by a senior government minister in the course of duty.

Actions for criminal libel are now rare: they are usually concerned with libels thought likely to create a breach of the peace.

Managers

Managers responsible for the day-to-day conduct of a company's affairs are regarded as agents: their legal liability is based on the law of tort, in particular of negligence, and on the law of contract.

A manager is employed under a contract of employment, which determines his duties and responsibilities within a company. If a manager is incompetent or negligent, the company can sue him for breach of contract; this seldom happens.

- A manager must perform his duties with the care expected of a reasonable man in his position and always act with good faith and honesty.
- Managers are not liable on contracts made by them on behalf of their companies. They could be liable for exceeding their authority to make contracts.
- A manager has all the rights of an employee against his company. He is entitled to be indemnified against liabilities or expenses incurred in the proper exercise of his duties.
- If a manager takes part in a negligent act, when acting on behalf of his company, he will be liable together with the company, to a person injured by the act. It would be no defence to say he did not know he was being negligent.

Negligence

If a manager's negligence causes harm to an outsider, such as a customer or supplier, the law of tort applies. The manager's liability will depend on whether he has been proved legally negligent in the performance of his duties. An injured third party will be able to recover compensation if he can satisfy the court that:

(1) the manager was under a duty to avoid harming him. The law imposes on everybody a duty to avoid harm to any other person who is in such a relationship to him that his acts or omissions are likely to harm him;

(2) the duty to take care was broken by what the manager did, or omitted to do. This means that the manager's conduct is compared with the standard of care that a court considers appropriate in the circumstances. In general, a professionally trained manager will be held to a higher standard than an unqualified one;

(3) he suffered some damage from a breach of the standard of care.

A third party who proves these three requirements may also sue the company if the manager's negligence arose in the course of his employment, on the grounds that the manager is an agent of his employer. Both agent and principal are liable for a tort; in practice it is the company that is most likely to be sued.

In general, the law recognises that it would be impracticable to provide that everybody injured or whose property is damaged by all negligent acts or omissions receives compensation. It, therefore, operates to limit the range of complaints. The law requires that, to be successful, an action for negligence should be made by persons whom the defendant should reasonably have in mind before committing an act or omitting to commit an act. The law applies both to negligent acts and negligent mis-statements. Where injury is suffered by a person acting (or failing to act) on a mis-statement made by a professional person or somebody with expert or special knowledge, an action for negligence may be successful.

Occupiers of premises who invite visitors are required to take care that the visitors will be reasonably safe for the purposes of their visit. Warning a visitor of possible injury or damage to property is not, by itself, taken as relieving the owner of the premises of liability. However, a visitor who knows of a risk in entering premises, and who willingly accepts that risk, will have no claim if injury results.

Motorists

The Road Traffic Act 1972 makes it an offence to drive, attempt to drive, or be in charge of a motor vehicle in a public place when unfit to do so as a result of consuming alcoholic drink or drugs (which can include those prescribed by a doctor).

The onus of proving that he was not driving or in charge of a vehicle is on the person accused. In general, he will need to establish either that the vehicle was incapable of being moved from its position, or that he had taken positive steps for somebody else to take control of the vehicle.

If he is in the vicinity of the vehicle and has the ignition key in his possession, he will be held to be in charge of it. Anyone supervising a learner-driver is always held to be in charge of the vehicle; however, a motor mechanic repairing a vehicle would not be deemed to be in charge, even if he were under the influence of drink or drugs.

In addition to these provisions, it is an offence under the Act to drive, attempt to drive or be in charge of a vehicle when the proportion of alcohol in the blood of the accused exceeds 80 milligrams per 100 millilitres of blood (or 107 mg of alcohol per 100 ml of urine).

A police officer in uniform is empowered to ask anyone he suspects of driving, or being in charge of, a vehicle while under the influence of drink to undergo a roadside breath test. Refusal to do so, without reasonable excuse, carries a fine. If the police officer, as a result of the test, believes the accused to be over the limit, he may arrest the suspect – even if he refuses to take the test.

At the police station, the law requires that the accused must be given the opportunity of taking a further breath test. If he declines, he may then be asked to provide a specimen of either his blood or his urine for testing in a laboratory. A police officer requesting specimens must offer the accused part of the specimens taken. The officer is also required to warn the accused of the consequences of declining to provide a laboratory specimen.

In all cases involving conviction of driving while under the influence of drink, endorsement of the accused's licence is mandatory.

Driving offences

The Road Traffic Act, 1972, lists three major driving offences:

(a) causing death by reckless driving;
(b) reckless driving; and
(c) careless or inconsiderate driving.

To be caught by this section of the Act, death from reckless driving must occur within a year and a day of the accident.

A court will decide on what constitutes reckless driving but is likely to give full consideration to a plea claiming a mere error of judgment or to an action caused by a driver's sudden illness or being hit by a stone thrown up by another vehicle.

A court will also decide what constitutes careless or inconsiderate driving after due consideration of evidence.

Parking

The main offences are:

• causing or permitting a vehicle to remain at rest in a position likely to cause danger to other persons using the road;
• fraudulently interfering with a parking meter, including inserting coins other than legal tender;

187

Essential Facts for Managers

- causing or permitting a vehicle to create an unnecessary obstruction.

Driving slowly does not create an obstruction, within the meaning of the Act. The owner of a vehicle may stop outside his house to load or unload the vehicle, or for the purpose of access.

Road accidents

The driver of any vehicle (including horse-drawn ones) involved in an accident must, if injury or damage results, (a) stop and (b) give his name and address (or the vehicle owner's name and address) to anybody who reasonably needs the information. This requirement applies only when:

- somebody other than the driver is injured;
- the other vehicle(s) involved is/are damaged;
- certain animals (including horses, cattle and dogs) are injured.

Irrespective of whether or not the required information has been given on the spot, the driver must report the accident to the police within 24 hours.

Patents

To be awarded a patent (*letters patent* in its older form), the applicant must establish that the product concerned is better in some substantial way than anything else made previously by somebody else.

Being better is not necessarily enough: the extent to which a new product is better than anything else is taken into account by the Patent Examination Officer handling the application. In practice, a company developing a product with some minor improvement over competing companies' products would be likely to find the effort and cost of obtaining a patent not worthwhile. It might, in any case, find it difficult to persuade the Examination Officer that the improvement was sufficiently important to warrant the award of a patent.

Consequently, the importance of a new product is a critical factor in deciding on an application for a patent. The inventor of a chemical process that transmutes lead into gold, for example, would probably have no difficulty in persuading the Examination Officer of the importance of his process. More prosaically, inventions such as the jet engine and zip fasteners clearly represent major advances in their respective areas.

Applying for a patent

The basic steps are:

- A description, which need not be detailed, is sent to the Patent Office with a request for the grant of a patent. The description need only be enough to identify the subject matter of the new product and the degree of novelty and inventiveness it embodies.

- If the Patent Office accepts the preliminary application it will issue a priority date (normally the date of the application). This gives the applicant protection against any requests made after that date for a similar product.
- The Patent Office then requires a specification, sufficiently detailed to enable someone skilled in the area served by the product to make it.
- The applicant is also required to submit his claims for the new product, specifying the protection sought. A further requirement is a short abstract of the scope of the product – sufficient to identify it readily.

For a period of 12 months from the priority date he has been allocated, the applicant is free to work further on his new product, and to publicise it, if he wishes, in the knowledge that he is protected against somebody trying to forestall him. Within the 12 months period, the applicant must decide if he wants to proceed. If he does, the consequences are:

- an examination officer will make a preliminary examination and search to establish whether or not a similar invention exists and whether or not the product is patentable;
- the examining officer will then issue a search report to the applicant who then has to decide whether or not to withdraw in the light of the report's findings;
- if he does not withdraw within a reasonable time, details of the new product will be published in the Patent Office Journal and will then become public knowledge;
- thereafter, it is for the applicant to request a substantive examination: a patent will then be either granted or refused.

A patent can last for 16 to 20 years, providing renewal fees are paid.

These procedures apply to new British patents. Old patents — pre-1977 — have a slightly different set of rules; in addition, provisions now exist to apply for both an EEC and a European patent.

Police powers

An arrest without a warrant may be made by either a private individual or by a police officer. The police officer, however, has more authority and protection than a private individual. A private individual making an arrest without warrant must:

- be reasonably sure or reasonably suspect that the person arrested is in the act of committing an arrestable offence;
- be reasonably sure that the person arrested is guilty of having committed an arrestable offence.

Essential Facts for Managers

A police officer is required by law to arrest anyone on the same grounds as those applying to an arrest by a private individual. In addition, he is required to arrest without warrant anyone whom he reasonably suspects (possibly on information given him by others) of having committed an arrestable offence, or anyone whom he reasonably suspects of being about to commit an arrestable offence. Anybody arresting another person must take him before a magistrate as soon as is reasonably possible.

An arrest warrant may be executed by anybody to whom it is addressed (in England and Wales) or by a police officer in the area in which he is serving. A police officer making an arrest under warrant need not have it in his possession, but must produce it as soon as he can if the person arrested asks to see it.

A police officer may break open doors in order to arrest somebody under warrant, but he must first tell the person to be arrested that he is a police officer with an arrest warrant and give reasonable time to allow admission.

Judges' Rules

The Judges' Rules govern the procedures which police officers may use in questioning arrested or suspected persons. They are not enforced by law, but departure from the code embodied in the Rules may result in a court rejecting evidence so obtained.

The main points in the Rules are listed below:

- A police officer seeking to find out if an offence has been committed, and by whom, may question anybody whom he thinks may have useful information relating to the alleged offence.
- When the police officer believes he has reasonable grounds for suspecting a person to be guilty of an offence, he must warn that person before he questions him further on the alleged offence.
- The warning should take the form: 'Do you wish to say anything? You are not obliged to say anything unless you wish to do so, but whatever you say will be taken down in writing and may be used in evidence.'
- If a person, after being warned, decides to make a statement, he may either write it himself or dictate it to a police officer. The police officer may not prompt or influence the person making the statement.
- The person making the statement must be shown the statement as written down and be given the opportunity to make any changes he wishes.

Aiding a police officer

Anybody refusing to help a police officer in the execution of his duty may be indicted for an offence, unless he is physically unable to do so.

190

Property

Because the sovereign is the ultimate owner of all land (in England and Wales), an individual or corporate entity can hold land only as the sovereign's tenant. In practice, however, the law provides full protection for anyone owning or acquiring land, thus effectively conferring full ownership.

Anyone having the absolute ownership of a piece of land is said, in law, to hold the fee simple of the estate. Absolute ownership conveys the right to enjoy the surface of the land, everything above the surface and any minerals beneath the surface. However, the law imposes a number of requirements.

- *Ancient lights.* The owner of a building is legally entitled only to the amount of light normally considered adequate to allow him or her to enjoy ownership of that building. If the light previously enjoyed is obstructed by a new building, the owner would need to prove either that the new building would lessen the value of his property or that it would materially affect his convenience, before obtaining redress.

- *Fences.* There is no legal requirement for the owner of land to fence against a neighbouring owner, or against a public highway. Anyone keeping animals on his land is, however, required to take reasonable care, by fencing or other means, to prevent them straying onto the public highway.

- *Overhanging fruit trees.* If a fruit tree overhangs a neighbour's land, the tree's owner has a right to require the return of any fruit that may fall on the neighbour's land.

- *Rivers and streams.* The owner of land through which a watercourse flows has a right to use water from it – unless it is in an area controlled by a River Authority. In such an area permission from the authority is normally required before using the river in any way. In tidal, navigable rivers, the soil belongs to the sovereign: in streams, where there is no ownership to the contrary, the soil belongs to the owner of the land through which it flows, or up to the centre of the stream, where it flows between two neighbouring lands not owned by the same person.

- *Roots and branches.* The owner of land may cut away, without giving notice, any roots or branches of trees which penetrate or overhang his land. He may not, however, enter his neighbour's land to do the cutting away without permission.

Buying and selling

Contracts for the purchase or sale of land, including houses, can be difficult and complex: conveyancing is not appropriate for d-i-y treatment. Some of the legal points are listed below.

- The buyer is the legal owner once the contract to purchase is signed by both parties. Whatever happens to the land and building(s) he must pay the purchase price: if he dies, the purchase price must be paid by his personal representative. Similarly, the vendor's representative must complete the sale.

* If either party fails to honour the contract to purchase, the other may either sue for damages or to compel performance. The contract can be enforced if it was reasonable at the time of signature even if it subsequently becomes unreasonable.

* A purchaser knowing of some latent advantage (the presence of valuable minerals, the granting of planning permission, for examples) in land and property is not required by law to advise the vendor. A purchaser may not, however, make misleading statements with the intent of persuading the vendor to reduce the purchase price

* A person who signs a contract for the sale of house and land after grossly misleading representations by the other party may be entitled to have the contract declared void.

* In all contracts of sale, certain conditions are implied:

    (a) the seller has the right to sell;
    (b) the land is free from encumbrances;
    (c) the buyer shall have 'quiet enjoyment'.

Trespass

A property owner has the right to use reasonable force to eject anyone who enters his property without permission. If, however, a trespasser leaves at once after being asked to do so, the owner will have to prove that the entry caused damage, before considering a suit against the trespasser. A simple suit for trespass, without damage being established, would be likely to win only nominal damages. In certain circumstances, a property owner might elect to enter such a simple suit in order to discourage others from trespassing.

Landlord and tenant

1 Business tenancies

The Landlord and Tenant Act 1954 provides security of tenure for tenants occupying premises for business purposes or for business and other purposes. A 'business' includes a trade, business or profession and any activity carried on by an incorporated or unincorporated body.

    A business tenancy may be terminated either by:

(a) service by the landlord of a notice to terminate; or
(b) service by the tenant of a request for a new tenancy.

Until terminated in one of these two ways, the existing tenancy continues beyond the original termination in the same terms as the original lease.

Landlord's notice to terminate

(a) The notice must be in writing and must specify a date of termination not earlier than the date on which the existing tenancy would have determined by effluxion of time or could have been terminated by notice.

(b) The notice must be given not more than 12 months nor less than 6 months before the termination specified in the notice, unless the terms of the existing tenancy require more than 12 months' notice to terminate, in which case the longer period of notice must be given.

Tenant's counter-notice

(a) The notice must be in writing and state that the tenant does not wish to give up occupation of the premises on the date of termination specified in the landlord's notice.

(b) The counter-notice must be served within two months of the giving of the landlord's notice to terminate.

On hearing the tenant's application, a court must order the grant of a new tenancy unless the landlord establishes one of the statutory grounds of opposition. These are:

(a) disrepair of the property due to the tenant's failure to perform his obligations;

(b) persistent unpunctuality in payment of rent;

(c) substantial breaches of covenant, other than as to repairs, or misuse or mismanagement of the premises;

(d) such suitable alternative accommodation has been offered as is available;

(e) the tenant's interest is a sub-tenancy of the premises and a letting or disposal of the whole premises would be prejudiced by the existence of a sub-letting;

(f) intended demolition or reconstruction;

(g) intended occupation wholly or partly for business purposes or as a residence by the landlord, or for business purposes by a company in which the landlord has a controlling interest.

Compensation

(a) *Compensation for disturbance:* if the landlord establishes one of grounds (e), (f) or (g) above, or if the tenant does not make or discontinues his application and no other ground has been stated in the landlord's notice, the landlord has no defence to an application by the tenant for compensation.

The amount of compensation is calculated by applying a multiplier to the rateable value of the premises. If the tenant or his predecessor have carried on the tenant's business for fourteen years or more before, the amount of compensation is calculated by applying the multiplier to twice the rateable value of the premises.

(b) *Compensation for improvements:* compensation for improvements must be awarded, whatever the ground of opposition established by the landlord.

A tenant may claim compensation only if, prior to making the improvement, he served on the landlord a notice in writing of his intention to make the improvement, together with a specification and plan.

The claim for compensation must be made in writing, stating:

- the name and address of the claimant;
- the landlord against whom the claim is made;
- a description of the premises and of the trade or business carried on there;
- the nature of the claim and particulars of the improvements, including the date they were completed and the cost;
- the amount claimed.

Where a notice to terminate is given by the landlord, the claim for compensation must be made within three months of the date of landlord's notice.

Where notice to quit is given by the tenant, the claim must be made within three months of the date of the landlord's counter-notice or (if no counter-notice is given) the latest date on which the landlord could have given a counter-notice.

Where the tenancy comes to an end by effluxion of time, the claim must be made not earlier than six months nor later than three months before termination of the tenancy.

The compensation must not exceed:

(a) the net addition to the value of the holding as a whole, which may be determined by the court to be the direct result of the improvement; or
(b) the reasonable cost of carrying out the improvement at the termination of the tenancy, subject to a deduction of an amount equal to the cost (if any) of putting the works constituting the improvement into a reasonable state of repair, except so far as such cost is covered by the tenant's liability under his repairing covenants.

2 Residential tenancies

The Rent Act 1977 provides security of tenure for tenants occupying certain premises under a protected or statutory tenancy. To qualify, the tenancy must satisfy these conditions:

- the tenancy must be contractual;
- the subject matter of the tenancy must be a dwelling-house let as a separate dwelling;
- the rateable value of the premises *on the appropriate day* must not exceed certain limits.

The rateable value limits

If the appropriate day fell before 22.3.73, the tenancy is a protected tenancy if the rateable value did not exceed any one of the following:

* £400 (London) or £200 (elsewhere) on the appropriate day; or
* £600 (London) or £300 (elsewhere) on 22.3.73; or
* £1,500 (London) or £750 (elsewhere) on 1.4.73.

If the appropriate day fell on or after 22.3.73 but before 1.4.73, the tenancy is a protected tenancy if the rateable value did not exceed any one of the following:

* £600 (London) or £300 (elsewhere) on the appropriate day; or
* £1,500 (London) or £750 (elsewhere) on 1.4.73.

If the appropriate day fell or falls on or after 1.4.73, the tenancy is a protected tenancy if the rateable value did not exceed: £1,500 (London) or £750 (elsewhere) on the appropriate day.

A rent must be payable of not less than two-thirds of the rateable value on the appropriate day.

Premises outside the Act

* Certain licensed premises
* Premises let at a rent inclusive of payments for board or attendance
* Tenancies where the rent is less than two-thirds of the rateable value
* Dwelling houses owned by the Crown
* Parsonages
* Premises leased by local authorities, development corporations and housing associations and trusts
* Student lettings by an educational body
* Certain holiday lettings
* Houses let with land other than the site
* Lettings by resident landlords
* Premises used partly for business purposes

Recovery of possession

If the landlord establishes a mandatory ground for recovery of possession, a court must make an order for possession, without considering whether or not it is reasonable to do so. The landlord must have given the prescribed notice, relevant to the case in question, that the possession might be required under that case.

* The landlord requires the dwelling-house as a residence for himself or any member of his family who resided with him as owner-occupier when he last occupied the dwelling-house as a residence, or the dwelling-house is required in certain other circumstances.
* The landlord intends to occupy the dwelling-house as his residence at such time as he might retire from regular employment and the landlord has let it on a regulated tenancy before he has so retired.

- The dwelling-house has been let under a tenancy for a term of years certain not exceeding 8 months and the dwelling-house was at some time within the period of 12 months ending on 'the relevant date' (which depends on the type of tenancy) occupied under a right to occupy for a holiday.
- A similar ground to the above exists in respect of a dwelling-house occupied by a person pursuing or intending to pursue a course of study. The tenancy must be for a term of years certain not exceeding 12 months.
- Church of England parsonages are excluded from the scope of the Act. Houses occupied by ministers of other denominations as a residence from which to perform their duties of office can be recovered under this ground.
- Possession can be recovered if the dwelling-house was at any time occupied by a person employed in agriculture and the regulated tenant from whom possession is sought is not, and never was, so employed by the landlord and is not the widow of a person so employed.
- The dwelling-house is required for occupation by a person employed or to be employed by the landlord in agriculture and is a farmhouse which was let on a regulated tenancy made redundant under a scheme of amalgamation approved under Agriculture Act 1967.
- The tenancy is a protected shorthold tenancy.
- Subject to satisfaction of certain conditions, possession may be obtained against a member of the regular armed forces of the Crown.

Apart from these mandatory grounds, a landlord may establish a discretionary ground for recovery of possession. However, a court will not make an order for possession unless it considers it reasonable to do so.

Discretionary grounds include:

- failure to pay rent;
- failure to honour obligations under a tenancy agreement;
- using the premises for immoral purposes;
- ill-treatment or neglect of the premises;
- sub-letting without the landlord's consent;
- the dwelling house is needed for occupation as a residence by: himself, any son or daughter over 18, his father or mother; his wife's father or mother.

Rates

The rateable value of a house, flat, private garage or private storage premises is normally calculated on an estimation of the annual rent at which the premises might reasonably be let if:

(a) the tenant pays the normal rates and taxes; and
(b) the landlord pays the cost of insurance and of keeping the premises in good repair.

Exempt from rates are:

- agricultural land and buildings;
- crown property, railways, harbours, canals and some property owned by the public utility services;
- police stations, lighthouses, churches, chapels and places of public worship.

In general, unoccupied premises do not attract a rates demand, but a local authority may impose a proportion of rates after a house or flat has been empty for over three months. If the owner of premises does not pay rates due anyone paying the owner rent for the whole or part of those premises may be required to pay rent normally paid to the owner to the local authority until the full amount of rates due is paid.

Public order

Riot

When three or more people, with a common purpose, clash violently with another group who oppose that purpose.

Affray

A display of force by one or more persons in a manner likely to frighten or intimidate a reasonable person.

Unlawful assembly

A gathering of three or more people for any unlawful purpose or any such gathering, for whatever purpose, where the public peace may be endangered.

Slander

Actions for slander (oral defamation) have a low success rate. This is chiefly due to the need imposed on the plaintiff to prove that he has suffered damage as a result of the slander. (In a libel action, the court assumes damage.)

The onus of having to prove damage is lifted, however, if the slander:

(a) accuses the plaintiff of having committed an offence punishable by imprisonment;
(b) disparages the professional or business activities of the plaintiff;
(c) accuses the plaintiff of having a contagious disease;
(d) suggests a female is unchaste.

7 The City of London

The City and its jargon

The City of London, as an international financial centre, is central to all economic activity in the UK. The behaviour of its markets, particularly the reasons for that behaviour, reflects developments in the economy on what is often a day-to-day basis.

Following those developments and interpreting them in terms of company planning is not easy. The City is a highly sophisticated centre made up of specialist technical markets, each with its own technical jargon.

However, the City's basic function is simple enough: it brings together people who want to borrow money with people willing to lend it, at a profit; or invest it, at a risk; or to speculate with it, at a greater risk but with hopes of a greater return.

Bill of exchange

Underlying this operation is an old friend: the bill of exchange. It is defined in law as:

> an unconditional order in writing, addressed by one person to another, requiring the person to whom it is addressed to pay on demand or at a fixed or determinable future time a sum certain in money to or to the order of a specified person, or to bearer.

This definition makes a bill of exchange a highly negotiable instrument. The rights and duties it creates can easily be transferred from one person to another. A bill of exchange is thus almost as good as cash in hand — provided, of course, that there is an acceptable guarantee that the payment it authorises will be made.

Such guarantees are provided by acceptance houses, which are merchant banks specialising in the business. The usual practice is to write the word 'accepted' on the back of the bill and sign it. Once so signed, the bill becomes a post-dated cheque, with payment guaranteed.

Discount houses

At this stage, the bill is sold to another specialist merchant bank — a discount house which pays the present value of the future amount payable, discounted at the prevailing rate of interest.

Discount houses are unique to London and play a significant part as intermediaries between the Bank of England and the commercial banks. The Bank is able, through discount houses, to influence the operation of the City's financial systems.

This is because the discount houses, in times of need, are able to turn to the Bank of England for funds: the Bank always makes the funds available, but at rates of its own choosing. The level of rates indicates the direction in which the Bank wants to see interest rates move generally.

It is from this fundamental and basic system that much of the jargon terms listed and defined below have sprung. The list is selective and includes only those terms most likely to be of use to management seeking to follow events with understanding.

Bond

A security paying a fixed rate of interest to the holder and (usually but not invariably) with a set date on which the borrower issuing the bond will repay the holder the full value of the bond as originally issued. Bonds are attractive to investors because they can be bought and sold easily: in normal times their market value fluctuates between narrow limits. In general, market forces act to keep the return to the investor in line with the level of interest rates generally. The bond market is thus not an area in which speculators — those looking for a capital gain through a sharp increase in the market value of a security — normally operate. The behaviour of bond prices is not particularly significant in company planning terms, unless a sustained trend either upwards or downwards develops. The reasons behind such a trend might then be an important factor in forward planning.

Blue chip

The share of a major, well respected and profitable company, which is often one of the market leaders in a particular field. The behaviour of the share price of a particular blue chip may be due to a variety of reasons, not all necessarily indicative of a wider implication. But a general movement of most blue chip shares will be reflected in the behaviour of the FT Industrial Share index. A sustained movement in either direction in that index is often a signal suggesting that a review of forward planning might be justified.

Certificate of deposit

A document issued by a bank to somebody depositing funds with that bank confirming that the deposit has been made. It is thus a negotiable instrument and can be bought and sold. The bank retains the deposit for the full term stated on the certificate (between three months and five years). CDs are relatively new: they first appeared in the United States in 1961 and were issued, in dollar terms, in London five years later.

Call

In general, call implies the demand by the issuer of money or equivalent for immediate repayment.

In the context of shares issued by a company, it may call for payment in full for the shares; or it may require payment by instalments. The normal practice is to require payment in full at the time of issue. In a banking context, call money applies to any funds placed by one institution with another on the understanding that they may be instantly withdrawn. Such funds are often placed by British banks with discount houses and money brokers to assist them with short-term needs. From the banks' point of view, call money helps them to comply with the Bank of England's monetary control requirements. A heavy demand for call money sustained over a period might signal an unusual situation, but would not necessarily be a danger signal.

Eurobonds

Medium- and long-term bonds, bearing a specified rate of interest, issued on the international financial markets in a currency other than that of the centre from which it is being issued. Such bonds are normally issued by governments, public bodies and major companies of international reputation and standing. Eurobond issues are for large amounts and require skilful handling. When issued by a government, it may be of interest to individual companies to know the purpose for which the money is being raised. If it is for some major capital project, there may be some business for an alert company to pick up.

Eurocurrency

Originally known as eurodollars or, sometimes, as petrodollars, the term is now used to mean any currency held by the owner in a bank outside the country issuing the currency. The eurocurrency market has grown strongly since the 1950s, when governments in Eastern Europe began to transfer their dollar holdings in American banks to banks in London as a precaution against having these holdings frozen during a period of strained relationships.

The growth of such transfers meant that banks increased their deposits and could thus increase their lending, mostly in short-term form. Many countries, particularly the less developed ones, found borrowing in the eurocurrency market was relatively easy. However, some of them over-borrowed and, because of the volatility of the market and the short-terms available, some borrowing countries found that they could not pay interest on due date — let alone the capital borrowed.

The total sums involved were so large that arrangements had to be made to ease the payments burden on the borrowing nations in order to avoid widescale default. If this had not been done, the results would have been very serious indeed for the international financial systems.

A particular feature of the eurocurrency market is that the funds are not easily controlled by national monetary authorities and there is concern about the growth of the market in general.

European Currency Unit

The ECU does not exist in the form of notes and coins but, as a vehicle for European trade and finance, it is becoming increasingly used.

It came into existence in 1979 as part of the European Monetary System which was formed to stabilise European currencies. Member currencies of the EMS (Deutschmark, French franc, Dutch guilder, Danish krone, Belgian franc, Italian lira, Irish punt and Luxembourg franc) are allowed to fluctuate within set bands on either side of their central rate.

The ECU is a weighted conglomerate — a basket currency — made up of fixed quantities of all the EEC member currencies with each constituent weighted. In sterling terms, the ECU is currently valued at around 60p.

Because the unit is much more stable against European currencies than sterling or the dollar, European countries are increasingly willing to be invoiced in ECUs. They are also increasingly used as the currency denomination of bond issues. ECU interest rates are determined by taking a weighted average of the component currencies' interest rates. As a result, an ECU-denominated bond is attractive to investors in low-interest rate countries (Germany and Switzerland) and to borrowers from high-interest rate countries (France and Italy).

Expectations theory

The belief is that the level of long-term interest rates reflects the views of investors on the likely level of short-term interest rates. If investors expect short-term interest rates to rise, they are likely to require a higher interest rate for investing long-term.

The belief is quite widely held and any widening or contracting of differentials between short and long rates could be worth further thought.

Financial ratios

Analysts and accountants use a range of financial ratios to assess the performance of individual companies. These ratios are not infallible — they do not take into account management style and other factors which cannot be expressed in terms of numbers. But they do provide a useful guide in measuring one company's performance against that of another in the same area of business.

Return on capital employed

The profit before taxation expressed as a percentage of the net investment in the business. It is a measure of the overall management of the company. The ratio permits comparison with both the performance of other companies in all fields and with the returns available generally in other forms of capital investment.

Trading return on net invested capital

The trading profit as derived from the trading activity itself, expressed as a percentage of the net capital invested in that activity. It isolates profit arising from the main trading activity of a company from revenue out of trade and other investments: and from exceptional items such as relocation costs, redundancy payments, the sale of a lease or building. It is thus a measure of trading efficiency, as distinct from the overall conduct of the company. These two ratios are primary ones. Because they are broadly based, they may mask unsatisfactory subsidiary trends in specific areas of a business. Other ratios are used for finer tuning.

Asset utilisation

The relationship between sales revenue and the assets directly employed to produce that revenue.

Current ratio

The relationship between current assets and current liabilities.

Debt collection period

Measures in days the collection period of credit account sales. Allowance has to be made for the fact that VAT is included in invoices, so that the true income from payments outstanding for payment is less, by the amount of VAT, than the invoiced figure show, within the 'accounts receivable' entry in a company's report and accounts.

Gearing — capital structure

Relationships between sources of long-term funding for the business. Too high a proportion of fixed-interest capital makes a company vulnerable to adverse trading conditions, since it must service the fixed-rate capital before determining a dividend. A consequence of this obligation may be a need to seek bank finance, thereby increasing the interest charge burden.

Essential Facts for Managers

Gearing — safety margin

Measures the relationship between shareholders' funds and liabilities to third parties. It permits an appreciation of the length of time a period of adverse trading conditions could be endured before full repayment of all liabilities to third parties would be endangered.

Gearing — interest cover

Measures the relationship between profit before tax (from which fund interest obligations are met) and the amount of interest payable. Given the variability of interest rate levels in recent years, this ratio helps to indicate the degree of fluctuation in current trading which would turn profit into loss.

Profit margin

Trading profit expressed as a percentage of sales revenue. The profit margin is a measure of management performance.

Stock turnover

The number of times a year stock is sold and replaced. In calculating this ratio, it has to be remembered that sales figures in published accounts include the profit mark-up: stock is shown in the books at cost.

Foreign exchange transactions

In their simplest form, these are the exchange of one currency for another at an agreed rate. These exchanges may be between one bank and another, or between a non-financial customer of a bank and that bank. International trade, investment and finance give rise to a huge volume of such transactions each day, and the 24-hour nature of money markets, and modern communications, means that there is a world market in such transactions.

Spot transactions

These are transactions in which the physical exchange of currency takes place as soon as practicable after the contract is made, and the rate of exchange agreed. This is by convention two business days after the contract, but by agreement can be sooner.

Forward transactions

These are transactions in which the physical exchange of currency takes place any time later than two business days after the contract is made. These can range from three days to one year ahead; there is a limited market in major currencies up to five years ahead.

Date option contracts

Spot and forward transactions generally fix the date on which the currencies are exchanged. This may not suit importers or exporters and others where the date of payment or receipt in respect of the underlying transaction is not certain. Under these circumstances most banks will agree to hold the rate open with their customers for a period of time (the 'date option') so that the transaction can take place any time during that period. However, the transaction *must* be completed at some time.

Put and call options

In these transactions, a bank will, for a fee, allow its customer to complete a foreign exchange contract or not, at the customer's option (the 'put' or 'call'). The option will extend only for a limited period, during which the customer must decide whether or not it wishes to complete the contract. Only a very limited number of commercial banks provide this service.

Currency swaps

These involve two foreign exchange transactions for the same currencies and for the same amounts, one effected spot, buying one currency for another, and the other for a fixed forward date, and selling the former currency for the latter currency. The effect is to 'swap' one currency for another for the period to the fixed forward date, and the technique is principally used in currency funding — swapping a liability in one currency for a liability in another — and hedging a currency exposure — offsetting a currency liability with a currency asset and vice versa.

Currency futures

The London International Financial Futures Exchange (LIFFE) provides, through its participants, which include a large number of commercial banks in London, the opportunity to purchase specific currencies for specific fixed forward dates in specific amounts ('currency futures'). It is less flexible than straightforward forward exchange transactions through a bank, but may obtain finer rates, and allow larger transactions to be effected without disturbing the level of the foreign exchange market as a whole.

Gold fixing

The price of gold is fixed twice a day between five bullion dealers in London. The level is determined according to supply and demand.

In broad terms, the gold market is dominated by two factors: supplies of gold reaching the market from the main supplier of new gold — South Africa;

207

and by the sale of gold from the Soviet Union. Both of these suppliers operate so as not to disturb the price level by heavy offerings at any one time.

However, gold is a traditional hedge for those who fear devaluation of a currency in which their holdings are held; or who, for a variety of reasons, think the gold price is due for an increase.

In general, a stable gold price is likely to indicate generally stable conditions in the financial markets. Rapid and sustained movements are worth investigation.

Investor ratios

- *P/E ratio*   Market price $\div$ Earnings x 100

  This ratio indicates how many years earnings at the current rate have been capitalised in the market price. A high ratio indicates expectations of continued growth.

- *Earnings per share*   Earnings $\div$ No. of Shares

  An improving EPS *augmented* by improving measures of return on capital employed is evidence of an astute plough-back and expansion policy.

- *Dividend yield*   Dividend $\div$ Market Price x 100

  A measure which indicates income yield. A high-rate taxpayer may wish to go for a low-income yield and high capital gain potential where capital appreciation is secured by the hire of expanding going concern value per share.

- *Dividend cover*   Earnings $\div$ Dividend
  A measure of the security of dividend payment under historical cost accounting conventions. Conversely indicates how much profit has been retained in the business.

LIBID

London Interbank Bid Rate — the rate at which a bank is prepared to borrow from another bank.

LIBOR

London Interbank Offered Rate — the rate at which a bank is prepared to lend to another bank.

The three-month LIBOR rate has developed into the major reference point for calculating the rates on much of bank lending.

Real rate of interest

The rate of interest on an investment, calculated by deducting the rate of inflation from the nominal interest rate. For example, a nominal interest rate of 12 per cent yields a real rate of interest of 6 per cent if inflation is running at 6 per cent.

Savings ratio

The proportion of savings to disposable income (income remaining after unavoidable bills — mortgages, rates, food, etc — have been paid). In general, the ratio falls during period of high inflation: this partly reflects a fall in the purchasing power of the £ and partly a preference to exchange disposable income for goods and services now, rather than save and see the purchasing power of savings erode because of inflation.

Movement in the ratio is of limited value as a guide to forward planning by companies. However, an underlying upwards movement over several years may be an indication of returning confidence in the growth of the economy as a whole and of a widespread acceptance that inflation is under control.

Treasury bill

Treasury bills are issued by the Bank of England, on behalf of the Government, to raise short-term (91 days) funds pending arrival of taxation payments from the economy.

There are two forms: tap and tender. Tap bills are issued to government departments temporarily holding large amounts of money and are not a significant market factor.

Tender bills are issued weekly by the Bank and are so called because the Bank announces the total of bills to be issued and invites tenders for them at a discount below the face value of the bills. The Bank repays in full in due course and the discount represents the return to the investing institution.

The operation, which has been running for over a century, is interesting in that bidders for the bills — financial institutions, with discount houses covering, by arrangement, the whole issue — indicate how much discount they think appropriate. The weekly tender is thus the market's view on the level of interest rates.

Finance houses

The financial markets available in the United Kingdom (chiefly, but not exclusively, in the City of London) divide broadly into four main areas: commercial banking; the stock market; the corporate finance market and specialist markets such as pension fund management, financial futures and insurance.

Commercial banking

Clearing banks (often called 'the clearers') have direct access to the clearing house arrangements through which all cheques are presented to the banks upon which they are drawn. The big four clearing banks based in London are Barclays, National Westminster, Lloyds and Midland: between them they account for some 85 per cent of all UK business. A further major group based in Scotland includes Williams and Glyn's, now merged with the Royal Bank of Scotland.

A main feature of all clearing banks is that they each have a large number of branches through which their services are widely available: they have a very large retail (individual account) business. Very few businesses do not have a clearing bank account, dealing, as often as not, through their local branch manager. But, with the increasing complexity of the financial products and services available, the clearing banks are now using senior managers outside the branch banking system to advise and handle the accounts of the larger corporate entities.

The basis of the business of a clearing bank remains the provision of three services: cash transmission; the acceptance of deposits and the provision of loans, usually of up to 10 years' maturity.

Merchant banks

The distinction between a clearing and a merchant bank is not easy to define. It has been said that a merchant bank is neither a merchant nor a bank and that it lives on its wits rather than on its deposits. It might be better said that merchant banks live on their specialist services rather than on any other banking activity. They have developed the greatest variety of financial services, principally for companies. They rely on their large commercial customers for their deposits and tend, therefore, to lend primarily to the corporate sector rather than to individuals.

Many merchant banks make funds available to corporate borrowers by way of acceptance credits, whereby the customer draws a bill of exchange (merely a post-dated cheque) on the merchant bank which then 'accepts it': it guarantees payment of the bill by due date. The bill is then sold to a discount house — another aspect of merchant banking — which will buy the bill for cash, charging a discount at the current rate of interest.

Corporate finance

With all banks competing strongly for business, the distinctions between merchant banks and the commercial banks are becoming increasingly blurred. All banks are likely to offer much the same range of services. But merchant banks are recognised as having the edge over commercial banks in several areas:

- managing syndicates of banks to provide funds for the larger companies;
- leasing, factoring;
- obtaining a Stock Exchange listing;
- leading international syndicated issues;
- identifying suitable acquisitions and mergers for their clients;
- managing pension funds and the funds of other savings institutions.

Rights issue

The most popular method for a company to raise long-term finance is the rights issue: it is thought its popularity will increase in the changing climate of the City of London. A rights issue involves the issue to existing shareholders in a company of new shares in proportion to their holdings. A typical rights issue might offer one new share for each four held.

The shares have to be offered at a discount: if they were not, shareholders wishing to increase their holdings in a company would do so in the open market. The bigger the proportion of new shares on offer, the bigger the discount will have to be.

The company will also have to allow a grace period, usually three weeks, so that shareholders can decide whether or not to take up the offer. If the price of existing shares falls in that period, it can ruin the issue; the discount offered may have to be substantial to offset that risk. An alternative is to have the issue underwritten, although that increases the costs of issuance by around 2 per cent and, in any case, the underwriters may only agree to support the issue if the initial discount appears large enough to ensure its success.

The timing of the rights issue is also very important — if the market is strong, then a company can raise a lot of money whilst its share price is high.

Large rights issues (over £3 million) require the consent of the government broker as to timing, and occasionally companies may have to queue. That can upset the success of the issue if market sentiment changes whilst the issue is in the queue; however, the queueing system does have its benefits since, if a lot of issues are brought to the market at the same time, investors can feel swamped and the outlook for all the issues can be dulled.

The Stock Exchange

The London Stock Exchange is the world's third largest, after New York and Tokyo. Over 7,000 securities are listed, including over 3,000 commercial and industrial securities.

211

The Stock Exchange has over 4,000 members who, until the 'big bang' of October 1986, were mostly brokers, acting as agents, buying and selling securities on behalf of their clients, with the remainder being jobbers, who acted as principals dealing in securities.

The big bang

The previous distinction between broker and jobber was abolished from October 26, 1986. There is now only one type of Stock Exchange member — a broker/dealer.

Some of these, called market makers, undertake to make markets (to buy and sell shares continuously under a strict code of practice); all are able to deal with the public. However, in any one deal the broker/dealer must tell the investor the capacity in which he is acting and cannot act in both simultaneously. Though the dealing system has changed, firms may continue to act only as the investor's agent, as the broker did previously.

To protect the investor, all information on trading and prices is stored and available for inspection later, to ensure that all deals are done to the best advantage of the investor.

The market in government stocks, the gilt-edged market, has also changed. There are now 28 firms of primary dealers, through which the Bank of England sells new issues. The primary dealers also deal in existing stocks, and make a market for other broker/dealers, who distribute shares to other investors.

Regulating the City

The Financial Services Bill, introduced to police the City after the big bang, gives power to authorise investment business to the Securities and Investment Board (SIB) in conjunction with the Organising Committee of the Marketing of Investments Board (MIBOC).

SIB will authorise and regulate investment businesses directly or recognise Self-Regulatory Organisations (SROs) to do so for it. SIB and the SROs will be central to the new regulatory framework.

Seven SROs are envisaged:

1   The Stock Exchange, which will regulate dealing and broking in securities, related options and futures, and incidental investment management and advice.
2   NASDIM, the National Association of Securities Dealers and Investment Managers, which will regulate dealing and broking in OTC securities, and investment management and advice in general.
3   AFBD, the Association of Future Brokers and Dealers, which will regulate

dealing and broking in futures and options and incidental investment management and advice.

4   ISRO, the International Securities Regulatory Organisation, which will regulate international dealing and broking in securities, futures and options, forward agreements and money market instruments.

5   IMRO, the Investment Management Regulatory Organisation, which will regulate investment managers and trustees of collective investment schemes (e.g. unit trust schemes and investment companies) and in-house pension fund managers.

6   LAUTRO, the Life Assurance and Unit Trust Regulatory Organisation, which will regulate life companies, unit trust managers and trustees in managing and selling insurance-linked investments.

7   LUTIRO, and Life and Unit Trust Intermediaries Regulatory Organisation, which will regulate insurance and unit trust intermediaries (i.e. brokers and consultants).

Listing

Having established itself in the commercial markets in which it operates and demonstrated an ability to generate regular profits, a company may consider widening the ownership of its shares by means of a public listing. A public listing brings certain clear advantages and benefits: it gives the company better access to sources of the capital which it may need to finance expansion, and greater flexibility in making acquisitions; it increases public awareness of the company, with possible benefits to its trading and commercial position; it provides a market for the shares of the owners of the company; it enables the company to create an employee share incentive scheme with permanently marketable benefits; it can avoid the disadvantages of a company being 'close' for the purposes of the UK tax regulations; and it may, if combined with an issue of new shares, enable the company to decrease its dependence on borrowings. These advantages will have to be weighed against the extra costs which will be incurred (both at the outset and from year to year), the high personal tax liabilities which may be incurred by the vendors, the exposure to the volatility of the market, to public scrutiny and to the risk of hostile take-over and the additional obligations to the new outside shareholders.

Marketability for shares in the UK can be obtained in three ways: through a full listing on the Stock Exchange, through the Unlisted Securities Market ('USM'), and through the 'over the counter' market.

Full listing

The main requirements for listing a company's share capital on the Stock Exchange are (i) for the company to have an estimated market capitalisation of at least £500,000 (although in practice a figure of at least £5m is normally more appropriate) and (ii) for at least 25 per cent of the class of share capital listed to be held in public hands. The listing requirements also include the preparation of an accountant's report in respect of the last five completed financial years and the publication of the full Prospectus in two national news-papers.

USM

This market was introduced by the Stock Exchange in November 1980 to provide a formal, regulated market, designed to meet the needs of those smaller, less mature companies which would otherwise not have been able to obtain access to the capital markets. There are three main differences in the requirements from those for a full listing:

- only a three-year trading history is necessary (five years for a full listing);
- companies can come to the USM so long as at least 10 per cent of the equity is in public hands (25 per cent for a full listing); and
- the advertising requirements are reduced (thus significantly reducing costs).

Companies on the USM may move up to a full listing by means of an introduction of the existing equity capital, usually at a time when at least 25 per cent of the company is in public hands, instead of by means of an offer for sale, which entails significant extra costs, particularly underwriting commission.

Over the counter market

Prior to the advent of the USM, a second tier market was started by a private bank, M.J.H. Nightingale & Co. Limited, to provide access to the capital markets and marketability for small companies. Nightingale (now called Granville & Co. Limited) acted as market maker, matching buyers and sellers of shares.

Shareholders

By becoming a member of a company, a shareholder enters into a contract with the company the terms of which are principally contained in the company's Memorandum and Articles of Association. The principal rights normally attached to shares comprise the rights to a dividend (*if declared*), to vote and to receive a return of capital upon liquidation. There are many other incidental rights including, for example, the right to receive a copy of the annual report and accounts. Many listed companies now offer their shareholders benefits in kind or discounts on the goods or services which they supply. Most shares fall into one of two classes, ordinary shares and preference shares. In addition, there are convertible debentures, a hybrid between debt and equity.

Shares in UK companies have a 'par' value (also called 'nominal' value), which is the monetary amount at which they are deemed to be fully paid. The most common par value for ordinary shares listed on the Stock Exchange is 25p, but shares with many different par values do exist. Shares can be issued at par value or any higher price but cannot be issued at less than par value. Shares can be issued fully or partly paid. Thus, for example a share of £1 par value could be issued at £1.50 paid. The balance of 50p is a debt to the company which may be called, generally, at any time in the future.

Ordinary shares

Ordinary shares are frequently referred to as 'equities' but also as 'risk capital', because the holders of them normally carry the main financial risk but also stand to receive the greatest potential rewards. They generally give the holders the right to appoint and remove directors, to receive dividends, if and when declared, and normally entitle the holders to exercise one vote for each share at general meetings of the company. Ordinary shares also usually give the holders the right to receive the due proportion of the company's assets in the event of it being wound up; otherwise they are not normally redeemable.

As with all shares, however, these rights may be modified by provisions in the company's Memorandum or Articles of Association and it is not uncommon for companies to have several different classes of ordinary share (typically entitled 'A' Ordinary, 'B' Ordinary, etc.), each with different voting rights.

These different rights can take a number of forms; for example, the 'A' shares might carry twice the number of votes per share as the 'B' shares, or they might carry the same number of votes but the votes would only be exercisable in certain specified circumstances. It is also possible to weight the voting rights so that, for example, small holdings carry larger (or smaller) voting rights per share than larger holdings.

Institutional investors, who are assuming an ever greater presence as shareholders in UK listed companies, dislike shares with no or restricted voting rights and it may, therefore, become increasingly difficult to launch successfully a new issue of such shares. There is now only a handful of companies with non-voting shares listed on the Stock Exchange and the Stock Exchange requires that all such shares must be clearly designated as non-voting.

Preference shares

Preference shares differ from ordinary shares in that they carry at least one preferential right (either as to dividend or as to return of capital on winding-up or both) over those attaching to ordinary shares. The rights attaching to preference shares typically consist of:

(a) the right to a fixed preferential cumulative annual dividend;
(b) the right, on liquidation, to repayment of the amount paid up on the shares in priority to repayment of the ordinary share capital, but no participation in any surplus; and
(c) voting rights only in specified limited circumstances, such as when the preference dividend is in arrears or a meeting has been convened for winding up the company.

There are many variations. The dividend, for example, is sometimes not cumulative but payable only if there are sufficient profits in the relevant year.

Some preference shares carry a fixed preferential entitlement to dividends and/or return of capital *and* a right to participate, along with the ordinary shareholders, in any dividends and/or return of capital in excess of the fixed preferential amount. Such shares are usually called 'participating preference shares'.

Listed conventional preference shares, that is those with the rights listed above, are normally valued in the market on a yield basis, unlike listed ordinary shares, whose value normally reflects, principally, the market's view of the future earnings potential of the company concerned. The yields available from listed preference shares reflect the yields available from comparable forms of investment, such as long-dated Government securities.

The main financial implication of a preference share issue is the continuing priority charge on the issuing company's earnings in meeting the preference dividend. It is seen as a sign of severe financial weakness for a company to 'pass' the dividend on its preference shares. Companies wishing to raise finance through the issue of preference shares therefore need to be confident that the preference dividend can be easily covered.

Preference shares can be a useful means for owners of successful private companies to realise part of their investment in the company without reducing the degree of control they exercise over the business. This can be achieved by a bonus issue of non-participating, non-voting shares to the existing shareholders, who then immediately sell the shares to institutional investors for cash.

Even listed companies, which are family controlled and wish to remain so, can take advantage of this route by issuing preference (rather than ordinary) shares under a bonus or rights issue. The family holders can then sell their preference shares or not take up their rights without running any risk of reducing their control of the company. Sometimes such issues are underwritten, in the case of a rights issue, or, in the case of a bonus issue, underpinned by a merchant bank offering to acquire any preference shares which the ordinary shareholders do not wish to retain.

Most preference shares are irredeemable (other than on liquidation), but some are redeemable and a few are convertible into other securities, such as equity. As with ordinary shares, it is possible to constitute preference shares bearing an enormous variety of different rights.

Convertibles

Convertibles are essentially a hybrid of debt and equity, in that they are normally securities issued in the form of unsecured loan stock, which are convertible, at the holder's option, into ordinary shares during specified periods. Before conversion, they will carry a predetermined interest rate. After conversion, they will normally thereafter be entitled to dividends at the same rate enjoyed by the ordinary shareholders. As with most securities, many variations exist; it is possible, for example, to create a convertible, which will automatically convert in certain circumstances (e.g. if the company concerned is acquired by another company), or which will convert into preference shares, rather than ordinary shares.

As they are normally issued in the form of convertible unsecured loan stock, many of the features of conventional (non-convertible) loan stock will apply to them. They will, for example, normally be governed by a trust deed and a trustee and there will usually be restrictions imposed on the company's borrowing powers and ability to change the nature of its business whilst any of the stock is still extant.

Stock Exchange requirements with regard to convertibles include the requirement that such stocks should be designated 'convertible' and that the company into whose ordinary shares (or other security) the stock is convertible should maintain sufficient authorised and unissued ordinary shares (or other relevant security) to cover all outstanding conversion rights.

After a holder of a convertible has exercised his conversion rights, he will become a member of the company and will normally be entitled to all rights enjoyed by the holders of ordinary shares in the company.

Warrants

A warrant gives the holder the right to purchase a given number of shares at a set price (in excess of the current share price) on or before a set date. Warrants are often issued as part of a package of other securities, such as loan stock. A loan stock with warrants attached therefore, like the convertible, represents a hybrid of debt and equity.